AF415217

Crafting Games with Python

From Basics to Brilliance

JARREL E.

Copyright © 2023 by Jarrel E.

All rights reserved. No part of this publication may be reproduced, stored or transmitted in any form or by any means, electronic, mechanical, photocopying, recording, scanning, or otherwise without written permission from the publisher. It is illegal to copy this book, post it to a website, or distribute it by any other means without permission.

Jarrel E. asserts the moral right to be identified as the author of this work.

Designations used by companies to distinguish their products are often claimed as trademarks. All brand names and product names used in this book and on its cover are trade names, service marks, trademarks and registered trademarks of their respective owners. The publishers and the book are not associated with any product or vendor mentioned in this book. None of the companies referenced within the book have endorsed the book.

First edition

Contents

Foreword

Introducing to you, with great pleasure, the extensive book "Crafting Games with Python." Python is a powerful and adaptable language in the world of computing, and this book is a must-have for anyone hoping to get into the fascinating field of game development.

The appeal of creating video games never goes away, drawing in both experts and hobbyists with the advancement of technology. The need for a comprehensive yet approachable guide that not only clarifies the complexities of Python but also offers a clear path for creating captivating and immersive games has led to the creation of this book.

Preface

Not only has Python become a very useful tool, but it's also a doorway into the fascinating world of game development. With great pleasure, I introduce this thorough reference, "Crafting Games with Python," which tries to demystify the art and science of creating games with the Python computer language.

This book is the result of a deep passion for both gaming and programming. I set out to build a thorough tutorial that would be useful to both novice and experienced developers after seeing the lack of a resource that could combine the strength of Python with the complexities of game development.

This book is organized to walk readers through the fundamental ideas of both game development and Python programming in a logical manner. Every section is carefully designed to expand on the information covered in the sections that came before it, making for a seamless and engaging educational experience.

Acknowledgement

Crafting Games with Python is the result of a team effort, and I would like to express my heartfelt appreciation to all of the people who have helped make this book possible. Their knowledge, assistance, and commitment have improved the content and guaranteed the caliber of the finished product.

Sincerely appreciate the technical reviewers' thorough analysis of the material. Their advice and observations have been invaluable in improving the content's technical precision and readability.

I would especially want to thank the editorial staff for their professionalism and meticulous attention to detail, which have made the final product much more polished and coherent.

I would want to express my gratitude to my family and friends for their consistent support and encouragement during this attempt, as well as for their patience and belief in the project's value.

Finally, I would want to express my sincere gratitude to all of the readers who have chosen to start this educational trip with "Crafting Games with Python." The spirit of this book is driven by your enthusiasm for game development and your curiosity.

Introduction

Python is a very flexible and approachable language that offers a welcoming environment for fans to go from basic ideas to the highest level of genius in game design. This series is not only a list of guidelines; rather, it is an exploration of the complexities involved in creating virtual worlds, with each chapter serving as a springboard for proficiency.

We explore the fundamentals of Python game development as we set out on our journey, revealing the ease of use and creative potential that Python offers. Every aspect, from the fundamentals of game design to the nuances of handling visuals and multimedia, is carefully investigated, providing the foundation for future expertise.

The adventure takes us through the visual storytelling tapestry, where animated static is given life, sprites come to life, and user interfaces fluidly lead users through immersive experiences. By combining human interaction, sound effects, and music in a harmonious whole, we create stories that captivate the senses in addition to games.

This project's investigation of game logic and algorithms is its central focus. We turn lines of code into dynamic, interactive environments by delving into the complexities of decision-making, collision detection, and artificial intelligence integration. Optimization becomes a main point, balancing visual aesthetics and performance in a nuanced way.

Along the way, testing and debugging become indispensable allies, guaranteeing the dependability and usefulness of our products. We optimize our code using optimization techniques so that it performs flawlessly and captivates players on a variety of platforms.

Crafting Games with Python is an invitation to go off on a life-changing journey rather than merely a manual. This series is an invaluable resource for anyone interested in learning more about game creation, regardless of experience level. It provides a thorough, accurate, and often humorous explanation of the many facets of Python game programming.

Now, let's get started on this journey from fundamentals to mastery, where every section represents a brushstroke and every line of code represents a stroke in the magnificent work of Python game creation. Greetings from the realm of art and science that creates games that go beyond the screen and make a lasting impression on the imagination.

Overview of Python in Game Development

Python proves to be an intriguing and versatile language that lets developers of all skill levels achieve their imaginative goals. Let's start by examining Python's role in game development for your series, "Crafting Games with Python: From Basics to Brilliance," before delving deeper into this dynamic area.

The Allure of Python: Python's simplicity, readability, and versatility are what make it so appealing in the game industry. Python is a high-level programming language that can be used by both novice and expert developers because it allows them to express concepts in fewer lines of code than lower-level languages. Because of its pseudo-code-like syntax, coding with it is more intuitive and natural.

Python Ecosystem for Games: Python has a robust ecosystem of libraries and frameworks, which are the foundation of its skill in game creation. Among the many notable Python modules for creating video games is Pygame, which is compatible with multiple platforms. Pygame offers features for graphics, sound, and user input, simplifying many elements of game development and laying the groundwork for creating entertaining games.

Versatility Across Genres: Python's adaptability may be applied to a wide range of game genres, including intricate simulations and 2D platformers. Because of its versatility, developers can make a wide variety of games, including complex simulations, puzzle adventures, and arcade games with a nostalgic feel. Python's versatility makes it a language that can be used to solve a wide range of creative needs in the game industry.

Rapid Prototyping and Development: Python is a great option for prototype and iterative design because of its flexibility and quick development speed. Python's short turnaround time is often appreciated by game creators, who can experiment with ideas, fine-tune game systems, and quickly implement improvements. A key component of refining and polishing game designs is this iterative process.

Community Support and Documentation: A big part of Python's strength in game development comes from its large documentation and vibrant community. With so many tools, tutorials, and forums at their disposal, developers may work together to solve problems and exchange expertise in a collaborative atmosphere. Anyone interested in studying Python game development will find that the learning curve is accelerated by this support architecture.

Cross-Platform Compatibility: The cross-platform interoperability of Python guarantees that games created with it will function flawlessly across a range of operating systems. This feature makes games more playable and expands their audience without requiring significant platform-specific adaptations.

Integration with Other Technologies: Python's strength in game creation stems from its ability to integrate with various languages and technologies. Python is a versatile canvas that can be used to create complex game experiences, whether you want to use it for AI aspects, integrate multimedia elements seamlessly, or use machine learning for specific tasks.

Goals and Structure of the Book

This book's primary goal is to provide readers with a clear, step-by-step guide that will take them from the fundamentals of Python game creation to the highest level of creative brilliance. The show's structured narrative attempts to support both novice and expert game developers as they delve into the intriguing field of game creation.

Foundational Exploration: The book's first few chapters concentrate on building a strong foundation. The fundamentals of Python as a language for developing games will be covered in detail, and readers will acquire a sophisticated grasp of the language's syntax, guiding principles, and thriving ecosystem. Principles of game design, managing graphics, and integrating multimedia will all be carefully examined, providing the foundation for the genius that will come.

Hands-On Implementation: With a practical approach to learning, the course expands on the fundamental information. The focus is on practical application, with readers working on projects, coding exercises, and real-world examples. This creates a dynamic learning environment that goes beyond theory and enables real-time, practical skill improvement.

Progressive Complexity: The structure of the book follows a carefully curated progression of complexity. Starting with simpler concepts, readers gradually ascend through the intricacies of game logic, algorithm implementation, and optimization techniques. This structured ascent ensures a smooth learning curve, allowing individuals to master each concept before progressing to more advanced topics.

Creative Exploration and Brilliance: As the series progresses, the focus switches to encouraging artistic experimentation. Readers will be guided through the process of creating their own games, experimenting with special features, and adding a dash of genius to their works. In addition to teaching readers technical skills, the book seeks to ignite their creative spark and enable them to imagine and create games that go beyond the norm.

In-Depth Topics and Specialized Insights: Some sections include in-depth analyses of particular subjects, offering expert insights into fields like artificial intelligence in video games, cross-platform issues, and sophisticated optimization techniques. These sections act as cornerstones of knowledge, strengthening the reader's toolkit and giving them the assurance to take on challenging tasks.

Iterative Learning and Reflection: The book promotes an iterative approach to learning, stressing the value of going over material again and taking stock of one's development. Readers are encouraged to solidify their learning with recurring summaries, challenges, and reflection tasks, strengthening their command of Python game development and getting them ready for the next phases of their adventure.

Holistic Mastery: This book's ultimate objective is to promote comprehensive mastery. By the end of the series, readers will have a strong technical foundation in Python game development as well as the problem-solving and creative abilities needed to make games that stand out in the crowded market for digital entertainment.

Python Game Development Fundamentals

Understanding Game Loops

The idea of a game loop provides the basis to the complex process of creating video games in Python. It is like a heartbeat that controls the game's progression and coordinates the player's interactions with the virtual world. Let's explore the fundamentals of game loops, dissecting their importance and provide useful examples to shed light on how they should be used.

The Essence of Game Loops: A game loop is essentially an endless cycle that controls a game's updating, rendering, and input processing. It makes sure the game runs smoothly by responding to player input, updating the state of the game, and producing the graphics at a steady pace. In order to create games with responsive and captivating gameplay, it is essential to comprehend the structure of a game loop.

Example of a Simple Game Loop in Python:

```python
import pygame
import sys

# Initialize Pygame
pygame.init()
```

```python
# Set up the game window
window_size = (800, 600)
screen = pygame.display.set_mode(window_size)
pygame.display.set_caption("Simple Game Loop Example")

# Game loop
while True:
    for event in pygame.event.get():
        if event.type == pygame.QUIT:
            pygame.quit()
            sys.exit()

    # Update game state

    # Render visuals

    # Control the frame rate
    pygame.time.Clock().tick(60)
```

In this example:

- Pygame is initialized, and a window is set up.
- The game loop runs infinitely, handling events such as quitting the game.
- Inside the loop, there are placeholders for updating the game state and rendering visuals.
- The **pygame.time.Clock().tick(60)** controls the frame rate, ensuring the loop runs at 60 frames per second.

Separation of Concerns: A well-designed game loop frequently has distinct challenges. Rendering graphics and updating the game state are two different operations. For example, handling game logic, positioning adjustments, and player input processing could all be part of the update phase. The render phase is dedicated to providing a visual representation of the game's current state.

Example with Separation of Concerns:

```python
import pygame
import sys

# Initialize Pygame
pygame.init()

# Set up the game window
window_size = (800, 600)
screen = pygame.display.set_mode(window_size)
pygame.display.set_caption("Game Loop with Separation of
Concerns")

# Game loop
while True:
    for event in pygame.event.get():
        if event.type == pygame.QUIT:
            pygame.quit()
            sys.exit()

    # Update game state
    update_game_state()

    # Render visuals
    render_game_visuals()

    # Control the frame rate
    pygame.time.Clock().tick(60)
```

In this refined example, **update_game_state()** and **render_game_visuals()** are functions responsible for their respective tasks, promoting a cleaner and more modular code structure.

Adapting to Game Complexity: The game loop changes as a game's complexity increases. For example, in real-time strategy games or simulations, rendering may need complex graphical rendering techniques, while the update phase may include complex artificial intelligence computations.

It is essential for any Python game developer to comprehend and become proficient with the intricacies of game loops. It establishes the foundation for engaging experiences, dynamic gaming, and the genius that will be revealed in this book's later chapters.

Handling User Input

User input has a significant role in establishing how the player interacts with the virtual environment. Let's look at the subtleties of controlling user input, a crucial element that improves the responsiveness and engagement of games. We'll use a number of real-world scenarios to demonstrate the Python user input implementation.

Basics of User Input: A variety of activities, such as clicks, mouse clicks, and keyboard strokes, are included in user input. The Pygame module offers a handy interface for recording and handling user input events in Python game programming. In order to make responsive and dynamic games, it is essential to grasp the fundamentals of event management.

Example of Basic Keyboard Input:

```
import pygame
import sys

# Initialize Pygame
pygame.init()

# Set up the game window
window_size = (800, 600)
screen = pygame.display.set_mode(window_size)
pygame.display.set_caption("Basic Keyboard Input Example")

# Game loop
while True:
    for event in pygame.event.get():
```

```python
        if event.type == pygame.QUIT:
            pygame.quit()
            sys.exit()

        # Handle keyboard input
        if event.type == pygame.KEYDOWN:
            if event.key == pygame.K_LEFT:
                # Respond to the left arrow key
                print("Left arrow key pressed")

            if event.key == pygame.K_RIGHT:
                # Respond to the right arrow key
                print("Right arrow key pressed")
```

In this example:

- The game loop captures events using **pygame.event.get()**.
- The **pygame.KEYDOWN** event is used to detect when a key is pressed.
- Specific keys, such as the left and right arrow keys, are identified and can trigger corresponding actions.

Mouse Input Handling: An further aspect of user engagement is mouse input. Pygame enables developers to record mouse events, like button presses and motions, expanding the scope of actions that players can perform.

Example of Basic Mouse Input:

```python
import pygame
import sys

# Initialize Pygame
pygame.init()

# Set up the game window
window_size = (800, 600)
screen = pygame.display.set_mode(window_size)
```

```python
pygame.display.set_caption("Basic Mouse Input Example")

# Game loop
while True:
    for event in pygame.event.get():
        if event.type == pygame.QUIT:
            pygame.quit()
            sys.exit()

        # Handle mouse input
        if event.type == pygame.MOUSEBUTTONDOWN:
            if event.button == 1:
                # Respond to left mouse button click
                print("Left mouse button clicked")

        if event.type == pygame.MOUSEMOTION:
            # Respond to mouse movement
            print("Mouse moved to", event.pos)
```

This example demonstrates detecting mouse button clicks (**pygame.MOUSEBUTTONDOWN**) and responding to mouse movement (**pygame.MOUSEMOTION**).

Combining Keyboard and Mouse Input: Games frequently need a combination of mouse and keyboard input. Both may be handled by the game loop with ease, giving the player a more satisfying experience.

Example of Combined Input Handling:

```python
import pygame
import sys

# Initialize Pygame
pygame.init()

# Set up the game window
window_size = (800, 600)
screen = pygame.display.set_mode(window_size)
```

```python
pygame.display.set_caption("Combined Input Example")

# Game loop
while True:
    for event in pygame.event.get():
        if event.type == pygame.QUIT:
            pygame.quit()
            sys.exit()

        # Handle keyboard input
        if event.type == pygame.KEYDOWN:
            if event.key == pygame.K_SPACE:
                # Respond to spacebar key press
                print("Spacebar pressed")

        # Handle mouse input
        if event.type == pygame.MOUSEBUTTONDOWN:
            if event.button == 1:
                # Respond to left mouse button click
                print("Left mouse button clicked")
```

This example showcases the integration of keyboard and mouse input handling within the same game loop.

To create visually striking, responsive, and immersive experiences in games, developers must have a solid understanding of and ability to leverage user input. Your skill with user input will help you design engaging games that provide players an engaging and dynamic gaming experience as you progress through Crafting Games with Python.

Introduction to Game Graphics

Virtual worlds are given life through the visual architecture of graphics. This section covers the foundations of game graphics and shows how Python may be used to create dynamic and graphically appealing games, especially when combined with the Pygame package. The fundamentals of game visuals will be clarified through real-world examples.

The Role of Pygame in Game Graphics: Pygame is a cross-platform collection of Python modules made specifically for creating video games, giving developers easy access to graphics management tools. Pygame offers a strong framework for creating visual tales, from handling visual elements to generating sprites.

Basic Drawing in Pygame: At the core of game graphics is the ability to draw on the game window. Pygame offers functions for drawing shapes, lines, and simple images.

Example of Basic Drawing:

```python
import pygame
import sys

# Initialize Pygame
pygame.init()

# Set up the game window
window_size = (800, 600)
screen = pygame.display.set_mode(window_size)
pygame.display.set_caption("Basic Drawing Example")

# Game loop
while True:
    for event in pygame.event.get():
        if event.type == pygame.QUIT:
            pygame.quit()
            sys.exit()

    # Clear the screen
    screen.fill((255, 255, 255))

    # Draw a red rectangle
    pygame.draw.rect(screen, (255, 0, 0), (50, 50, 100, 100))
```

```python
# Draw a blue circle
pygame.draw.circle(screen, (0, 0, 255), (200, 200), 50)

# Update the display
pygame.display.flip()
```

The output of this code is in the diagram below:

In this example:

- The game loop handles the quit event.
- The screen is cleared with a white background.
- A red rectangle and a blue circle are drawn on the screen.

· The display is updated to reflect the changes.

Loading and Displaying Images: Beyond simple sketching, complex pictures called sprites are frequently used in games. Pygame makes it easier to load and show picture files, which gives game graphics more nuance and complexity.

Example of Loading and Displaying an Image:

```python
import pygame
import sys

# Initialize Pygame
pygame.init()

# Set up the game window
window_size = (800, 600)
screen = pygame.display.set_mode(window_size)
pygame.display.set_caption("Image Display Example")

# Load an image
image = pygame.image.load("image.png")

# Get the image rect for positioning
image_rect = image.get_rect()

# Game loop
while True:
    for event in pygame.event.get():
        if event.type == pygame.QUIT:
            pygame.quit()
            sys.exit()

    # Clear the screen
    screen.fill((255, 255, 255))

    # Display the loaded image
    screen.blit(image, image_rect)
```

```
    # Update the display
    pygame.display.flip()
```

Here, the **pygame.image.load()** function is used to load an image file, and **screen.blit()** is employed to display it on the game window.

Animation and Sprite Movement: Sprites can have dynamic movement by having their positions updated over time through animation. Sprite animation and movement are made easier with Pygame.

Example of Sprite Animation and Movement:

```
import pygame
import sys

# Initialize Pygame
pygame.init()

# Set up the game window
window_size = (800, 600)
screen = pygame.display.set_mode(window_size)
pygame.display.set_caption("Sprite Animation Example")

# Load a sprite sheet or individual images for animation
sprite_image = pygame.image.load("sprite.png")

# Get the sprite image rect for positioning
sprite_rect = sprite_image.get_rect()

# Set the initial position
x, y = 50, 50

# Set the initial velocity
vx, vy = 5, 0

# Game loop
while True:
```

```python
for event in pygame.event.get():
    if event.type == pygame.QUIT:
        pygame.quit()
        sys.exit()

# Update sprite position
x += vx
y += vy

# Wrap around the screen
if x > window_size[0]:
    x = 0

# Clear the screen
screen.fill((255, 255, 255))

# Display the sprite at the updated position
screen.blit(sprite_image, (x, y))

# Update the display
pygame.display.flip()
```

In this example, the sprite's position is updated in the game loop, creating the illusion of movement. The sprite wraps around the screen to demonstrate continuous animation.

Learning Python game graphics opens the door to a world where code and creativity come together. As you work your way through this book, learning about game graphics will become essential to creating visually appealing and engaging games.

Setting Up Your Development Environment

Installing Necessary Tools and Libraries

Starting the development environment is the first step in the fascinating process of using Python to create games. The installation of necessary tools and libraries is walked through in this chapter to provide a seamless and effective beginning to the game production process.

Installing Python: Begin by installing the Python programming language, the foundation for game development. Visit the official Python website (https://www.python.org/) to download the latest version. Follow the installation instructions provided for your operating system.

Setting up a Virtual Environment: Create a virtual environment to isolate the dependencies of your game project. Open a terminal or command prompt and use the following commands:

For Unix/Linux/macOS:

```
python3 -m venv myenv
source myenv/bin/activate
```

For Windows:

```
python -m venv myenv
.\myenv\Scripts\activate
```

Replace "myenv" with the desired name for your virtual environment.

Installing Pygame: Pygame is a fundamental library for Python game development. Install it using the following command within your virtual environment:

```
pip install pygame
```

This command fetches and installs Pygame and its dependencies. With Pygame, you gain access to features like graphics rendering, sound, and event handling.

Example of a Simple Pygame Program: Create a simple Pygame program to verify the installation. Save the following code in a file (e.g., **simple_game.py**) and run it:

```
import pygame
import sys

# Initialize Pygame
pygame.init()

# Set up the game window
window_size = (400, 300)
screen = pygame.display.set_mode(window_size)
pygame.display.set_caption("Simple Pygame Example")

# Game loop
while True:
    for event in pygame.event.get():
        if event.type == pygame.QUIT:
            pygame.quit()
```

```python
        sys.exit()

    # Clear the screen
    screen.fill((255, 255, 255))

    # Draw a red rectangle
    pygame.draw.rect(screen, (255, 0, 0), (50, 50, 100, 100))

    # Update the display
    pygame.display.flip()
```

This program initializes Pygame, creates a window, and draws a red rectangle. Run the program to ensure Pygame is installed correctly.

Additional Tools for Development:

- **Code Editor or IDE:** Choose a code editor or integrated development environment (IDE) to write your Python code. Popular choices include Visual Studio Code, PyCharm, and Sublime Text.
- **Version Control System:** Consider using a version control system like Git to track changes in your code. Platforms like GitHub, GitLab, or Bitbucket provide hosting for your repositories.
- **Graphics and Audio Software:** Depending on your game's requirements, you might need graphic design tools like GIMP or Adobe Photoshop for visuals and Audacity or Adobe Audition for audio.

Configuring the Development Environment

A smooth and effective Python game development process depends on having a properly set development environment. As readers begin the process of using Python to create games, this section walks them through the necessary setups to guarantee a seamless workflow.

Virtual Environment: To isolate project dependencies, a conventional procedure is to create a virtual environment. By doing this, you can make sure that your game project has its own libraries without affecting the Python environment globally.

Open a terminal or command prompt and execute the following commands:

For Unix/Linux/macOS:

```
python3 -m venv myenv
source myenv/bin/activate
```

For Windows:

```
python -m venv myenv
.\myenv\Scripts\activate
```

Replace "myenv" with your preferred virtual environment name. Activating the virtual environment is essential before starting any development.

Installing Required Libraries: Install the necessary libraries for game development. In addition to Pygame, you might need other libraries based on your game's requirements. For example, for 3D graphics, you can use PyOpenGL.

```
pip install pygame
```

For PyOpenGL:

```
pip install PyOpenGL
```

Integrated Development Environment (IDE): Choose a suitable IDE or code editor for Python development. Popular choices include Visual Studio Code, PyCharm, and Sublime Text. These tools offer features like code highlighting, debugging, and version control integration.

Version Control: Implementing version control, typically with Git, is crucial for tracking changes in your codebase. Create a Git repository for your project and commit regularly. Platforms like GitHub or GitLab provide hosting for your repositories.

Example of Basic Git Commands:

```
git init  # Initialize a new Git repository
git add .  # Add all changes to the staging area
git commit -m "Initial commit"  # Commit changes with a
meaningful message
```

Project Structure: Organize your project into a structured directory layout. This improves readability and maintainability as your project grows.

Example Project Structure:

```
my_game/
|-- my_game/
|    |-- __init__.py
|    |-- main.py
|-- assets/
|-- venv/
|-- .git/
|-- README.md
```

Code Linting and Formatting: Adopt a consistent coding style by using a linter and code formatter. Tools like Flake8 and Black help ensure code quality and adherence to PEP 8 standards.

Example of Installing Flake8 and Black:

```
pip install flake8 black
```

EditorConfig: Create an **.editorconfig** file in your project to define and maintain consistent coding styles across different editors and IDEs.

Example **.editorconfig**:

```
# .editorconfig

root = true

[*]
indent_style = space
indent_size = 4
end_of_line = lf
charset = utf-8
trim_trailing_whitespace = true
insert_final_newline = true
```

Environment Variables: If your game requires configuration settings, consider using environment variables. The **python-dotenv** library simplifies the management of environment variables in your project.

Example of Installing python-dotenv:

```
pip install python-dotenv
```

In your Python code, load environment variables using:

```
import os
from dotenv import load_dotenv

load_dotenv()

API_KEY = os.getenv("API_KEY")
```

Python game development can be made more efficient and well-organized by setting up your development environment according to these best practices. As you move through the Crafting Games with Python book, you'll learn how to incorporate game mechanics, visuals, and interactivity in a well-configured environment.

Basic Game Development Concepts

Exploring Game Mechanics

Any engaging gaming experience is largely dependent on its game mechanics, which determine the interactions, laws, and dynamics of the virtual world. This chapter explores the fundamental ideas of game mechanics using Python, accompanied by real-world examples that shed light on how important principles are put into practice.

Player Input and Controls: Player input and controls are frequently where game mechanisms start. Pygame gives developers an easy-to-use method for recording user input so they may customize how players engage with the game.

Example of Player Input Handling:

```python
import pygame
import sys

# Initialize Pygame
pygame.init()

# Set up the game window
window_size = (800, 600)
screen = pygame.display.set_mode(window_size)
```

```python
pygame.display.set_caption("Player Input Example")

# Player position
player_x, player_y = 100, 100
player_speed = 5

# Game loop
while True:
    for event in pygame.event.get():
        if event.type == pygame.QUIT:
            pygame.quit()
            sys.exit()

    # Handle player input
    keys = pygame.key.get_pressed()
    if keys[pygame.K_LEFT]:
        player_x -= player_speed
    if keys[pygame.K_RIGHT]:
        player_x += player_speed
    if keys[pygame.K_UP]:
        player_y -= player_speed
    if keys[pygame.K_DOWN]:
        player_y += player_speed

    # Clear the screen
    screen.fill((255, 255, 255))

    # Draw the player
    pygame.draw.rect(screen, (0, 0, 255), (player_x, player_y,
    50, 50))

    # Update the display
    pygame.display.flip()
```

In this example, the player's position is updated based on keyboard input, allowing movement in different directions using the arrow keys as shown in the image below.

Collision Detection: A basic gaming mechanic that determines when in-game entities interact with one another is collision detection. Pygame has features that allow you to find collisions between forms.

Example of Simple Collision Detection:

```python
import pygame
import sys

# Initialize Pygame
pygame.init()

# Set up the game window
window_size = (800, 600)
screen = pygame.display.set_mode(window_size)
pygame.display.set_caption("Collision Detection Example")
```

```python
# Player position
player_x, player_y = 100, 100
player_width, player_height = 50, 50

# Obstacle position
obstacle_x, obstacle_y = 200, 200
obstacle_width, obstacle_height = 100, 100

# Game loop
while True:
    for event in pygame.event.get():
        if event.type == pygame.QUIT:
            pygame.quit()
            sys.exit()

    # Handle player input (similar to the previous example)

    # Simple collision detection
    if (
        player_x < obstacle_x + obstacle_width
        and player_x + player_width > obstacle_x
        and player_y < obstacle_y + obstacle_height
        and player_y + player_height > obstacle_y
    ):
        print("Collision detected!")

    # Clear the screen
    screen.fill((255, 255, 255))

    # Draw the player and obstacle
    pygame.draw.rect(screen, (0, 0, 255), (player_x, player_y,
    player_width, player_height))
    pygame.draw.rect(screen, (255, 0, 0), (obstacle_x,
    obstacle_y, obstacle_width, obstacle_height))

    # Update the display
    pygame.display.flip()
```

In this example, a simple rectangular collision detection mechanism is implemented, triggering a message when the player collides with an obstacle. See the output in the image below.

Game Logic and State Management: Creating dynamic and ever-evolving gaming experiences necessitates careful management of game logic and state. This covers level management, score keeping, and handling changes in game states.

Example of Game Logic and State Management:

```
import pygame
import sys

# Initialize Pygame
```

```python
pygame.init()

# Set up the game window
window_size = (800, 600)
screen = pygame.display.set_mode(window_size)
pygame.display.set_caption("Game Logic Example")

# Game state
score = 0

# Game loop
while True:
    for event in pygame.event.get():
        if event.type == pygame.QUIT:
            pygame.quit()
            sys.exit()

    # Handle player input (similar to the first example)

    # Update game logic
    score += 1

    # Clear the screen
    screen.fill((255, 255, 255))

    # Display the score
    font = pygame.font.Font(None, 36)
    text = font.render(f"Score: {score}", True, (0, 0, 0))
    screen.blit(text, (10, 10))

    # Update the display
    pygame.display.flip()
```

This example introduces a simple scoring system, incrementing the score in each iteration of the game loop and displaying it on the screen. See output below.

Game Logic Example   —   ×

Score: 1935

You establish the foundation for creating games that captivate and engross players as you investigate these essential game principles in Python. The examples given here provide as a springboard for more advanced and sophisticated game creation ideas that will be covered in later chapters of Making Games with Python.

Implementing Simple Game Logic

The intelligence of a game is derived from its game logic, which controls how it reacts to player input, changes over time, and produces an enjoyable user experience. This section examines how basic game logic can be implemented with Python, using real-world examples to highlight important ideas.

Scoring System: A scoring system gives games a sense of accomplishment and encourages participants to aim for success. Putting in place a simple scoring system is a great way to start learning game logic.

Example of a Scoring System:

```python
import pygame
import sys

# Initialize Pygame
pygame.init()

# Set up the game window
window_size = (800, 600)
screen = pygame.display.set_mode(window_size)
pygame.display.set_caption("Scoring System Example")

# Game state
score = 0

# Game loop
while True:
    for event in pygame.event.get():
        if event.type == pygame.QUIT:
            pygame.quit()
            sys.exit()

    # Handle player input (similar to previous examples)

    # Update game logic
    # Example: Increment the score every frame
    score += 1

    # Clear the screen
    screen.fill((255, 255, 255))

    # Display the score
    font = pygame.font.Font(None, 36)
    text = font.render(f"Score: {score}", True, (0, 0, 0))
    screen.blit(text, (10, 10))
```

```
    # Update the display
    pygame.display.flip()
```

In this example, the score is incremented every frame of the game loop, creating a continuous scoring experience. Output is similar to the previous example.

Time-Based Events: Introducing time-based events adds dynamism to games. It enables actions to occur after a certain duration, creating a sense of urgency or rhythm.

Example of Time-Based Events:

```
import pygame
import sys

# Initialize Pygame
pygame.init()

# Set up the game window
window_size = (800, 600)
screen = pygame.display.set_mode(window_size)
pygame.display.set_caption("Time-Based Events Example")

# Game state
score = 0
time_elapsed = 0

# Game loop
while True:
    for event in pygame.event.get():
        if event.type == pygame.QUIT:
            pygame.quit()
            sys.exit()

    # Handle player input (similar to previous examples)
```

```python
# Update game logic
# Example: Increment the score every frame
score += 1

# Increment time elapsed
time_elapsed += 1

# Perform an action after 100 frames (2 seconds at 50 frames
per second)
if time_elapsed == 100:
    print("Time-based event triggered!")

# Clear the screen
screen.fill((255, 255, 255))

# Display the score
font = pygame.font.Font(None, 36)
text = font.render(f"Score: {score}", True, (0, 0, 0))
screen.blit(text, (10, 10))

# Update the display
pygame.display.flip()
```

In this example, a time-based event is triggered after a specific number of frames, showcasing the concept of time-based game logic.

Win/Lose Conditions: Putting win/lose conditions in place gives one a feeling of challenge and success. It lets players accomplish goals and deal with repercussions for their choices.

Example of Win/Lose Conditions:

```python
import pygame
import sys

# Initialize Pygame
```

```python
pygame.init()

# Set up the game window
window_size = (800, 600)
screen = pygame.display.set_mode(window_size)
pygame.display.set_caption("Win/Lose Conditions Example")

# Game state
score = 0
health = 100

# Game loop
while True:
    for event in pygame.event.get():
        if event.type == pygame.QUIT:
            pygame.quit()
            sys.exit()

    # Handle player input (similar to previous examples)

    # Update game logic
    # Example: Increment the score every frame
    score += 1

    # Example: Deduct health if a certain condition is met
    if score % 500 == 0:  # Deduct health every 500 frames
        health -= 10

    # Check win/lose conditions
    if health <= 0:
        print("Game over! You lose.")
        pygame.quit()
        sys.exit()
    elif score >= 1000:
        print("Congratulations! You win.")
        pygame.quit()
        sys.exit()

    # Clear the screen
    screen.fill((255, 255, 255))
```

```python
# Display the score and health
font = pygame.font.Font(None, 36)
score_text = font.render(f"Score: {score}", True, (0, 0, 0))
health_text = font.render(f"Health: {health}", True, (255, 0,
0))
screen.blit(score_text, (10, 10))
screen.blit(health_text, (10, 50))

# Update the display
pygame.display.flip()
```

In this example, win/lose conditions are defined based on the player's score and health, demonstrating how game logic can lead to different outcomes. output shown in the screenshot below.

Win/Lose Conditions Example

Score: 208

Health: 100

By putting these straightforward examples of game logic into practice, you create the groundwork for more intricate and captivating gameplay. The complex game mechanics that will be revealed in the book's later chapters are constructed using the principles that are examined in this section.

Incorporating Basic Graphics and Sound

Essential elements that take a game from simple to immersive are graphics and sound. In this section we examine how to use Python to incorporate simple images and sound, providing real-world examples to show how to combine the two sensory aspects.

Basic Graphics with Pygame: A powerful framework for adding visuals to Python games is offered by Pygame. Pygame makes it easier to create visually appealing game pieces, from sketching shapes to displaying graphics.

Example of Basic Graphics:

```
import pygame
import sys

# Initialize Pygame
pygame.init()

# Set up the game window
window_size = (800, 600)
screen = pygame.display.set_mode(window_size)
pygame.display.set_caption("Basic Graphics Example")

# Game loop
while True:
    for event in pygame.event.get():
        if event.type == pygame.QUIT:
            pygame.quit()
            sys.exit()
```

```python
# Clear the screen
screen.fill((255, 255, 255))

# Draw a red rectangle
pygame.draw.rect(screen, (255, 0, 0), (50, 50, 100, 100))

# Draw a blue circle
pygame.draw.circle(screen, (0, 0, 255), (200, 200), 50)

# Update the display
pygame.display.flip()
```

In this example, a red rectangle and a blue circle are drawn on the screen, showcasing the basic drawing capabilities of Pygame.

Displaying Images: Enhance the visual appeal of your game by loading and displaying images. Pygame makes it easy to incorporate sprite graphics into your Python game.

Example of Displaying Images:

```python
import pygame
import sys

# Initialize Pygame
pygame.init()

# Set up the game window
window_size = (800, 600)
screen = pygame.display.set_mode(window_size)
pygame.display.set_caption("Displaying Images Example")

# Load an image
image = pygame.image.load("image.png")

# Get the image rect for positioning
image_rect = image.get_rect()

# Game loop
while True:
    for event in pygame.event.get():
        if event.type == pygame.QUIT:
            pygame.quit()
            sys.exit()

    # Clear the screen
    screen.fill((255, 255, 255))

    # Display the loaded image
    screen.blit(image, image_rect)

    # Update the display
    pygame.display.flip()
```

In this example, an image is loaded and displayed on the game window, demonstrating the integration of external graphics.

Adding Sound Effects: Sound effects improve the entire gaming experience by adding to the auditory aspect of the game. Sound may be easily added to Python games with Pygame.

Example of Adding Sound:

```python
import pygame
import sys

# Initialize Pygame
pygame.init()

# Set up the game window
window_size = (800, 600)
screen = pygame.display.set_mode(window_size)
pygame.display.set_caption("Adding Sound Example")

# Load a sound file
sound_effect = pygame.mixer.Sound("sound_effect.wav")

# Game loop
while True:
    for event in pygame.event.get():
        if event.type == pygame.QUIT:
            pygame.quit()
            sys.exit()

        # Play the sound effect on key press (e.g., spacebar)
        if event.type == pygame.KEYDOWN and event.key ==
        pygame.K_SPACE:
            sound_effect.play()

    # Clear the screen
    screen.fill((255, 255, 255))

    # Update the display
```

```
pygame.display.flip()
```

In this example, a sound effect is loaded and played when the spacebar is pressed, showcasing the incorporation of sound into the game.

Combining Graphics and Sound: For a seamless and engrossing gaming experience, combine sound and images. This example shows a situation when clicking on an object causes a sound effect to play.

```
import pygame
import sys

# Initialize Pygame
pygame.init()

# Set up the game window
window_size = (800, 600)
screen = pygame.display.set_mode(window_size)
pygame.display.set_caption("Graphics and Sound Example")

# Load an image
image = pygame.image.load("clickable_object.png")
image_rect = image.get_rect()

# Load a sound file
click_sound = pygame.mixer.Sound("click_sound.wav")

# Game loop
while True:
    for event in pygame.event.get():
        if event.type == pygame.QUIT:
            pygame.quit()
            sys.exit()

        # Check for mouse click
        if event.type == pygame.MOUSEBUTTONDOWN and event.button
        == 1:
            # Check if the click is on the clickable object
```

```python
        if image_rect.collidepoint(event.pos):
            click_sound.play()

# Clear the screen
screen.fill((255, 255, 255))

# Display the clickable object
screen.blit(image, image_rect)

# Update the display
pygame.display.flip()
```

In this example, a sound effect is played when the left mouse button is clicked on a clickable object, demonstrating the integration of graphics and sound.

You may build captivating, multi-sensory gaming experiences by experimenting with the integration of images and music in Python games. More sophisticated implementations will be covered in later chapters of this book, building on the examples given here.

Your First Simple Game Project

Creating a Basic Game Project

I'll walk you through the steps of making a simple bike racing game project in this chapter. From creating a prototype to creating the game itself, we'll go over the key phases with clear examples. The player is represented by the simple blue rectangle.

Define the Game Concept:

Before diving into code, define the concept of your bike racing game. Consider aspects like player controls, race tracks, obstacles, and scoring mechanisms.

Set Up the Project Structure:

Organize your project by creating a clear directory structure. This helps maintain a well-organized codebase.

Example Project Structure:

```
bike_racing_game/
|-- assets/
|    |-- images/
|    |-- sounds/
```

```
|-- src/
|    |-- __init__.py
|    |-- main.py
|-- .gitignore
|-- README.md
```

Build a Prototype:

Start with a basic prototype to test game mechanics. Focus on player movement and a simple representation of the race track.

```python
# main.py (Prototype)

import pygame
import sys

# Initialize Pygame
pygame.init()

# Set up the game window
window_size = (800, 600)
screen = pygame.display.set_mode(window_size)
pygame.display.set_caption("Bike Racing Game Prototype")

# Player position
player_x, player_y = 400, 500
player_speed = 5

# Game loop
while True:
    for event in pygame.event.get():
        if event.type == pygame.QUIT:
            pygame.quit()
            sys.exit()

    # Handle player input
    keys = pygame.key.get_pressed()
```

```python
    if keys[pygame.K_LEFT]:
        player_x -= player_speed
    if keys[pygame.K_RIGHT]:
        player_x += player_speed

    # Clear the screen
    screen.fill((255, 255, 255))

    # Draw the player
    pygame.draw.rect(screen, (0, 0, 255), (player_x, player_y,
    50, 50))

    # Update the display
    pygame.display.flip()
```

Refine Game Mechanics:

Iterate on the prototype to enhance game mechanics. Add visual elements like a road and improve player movement.

```python
# main.py (Refined)

import pygame
import sys

# Initialize Pygame
pygame.init()

# Set up the game window
window_size = (800, 600)
screen = pygame.display.set_mode(window_size)
pygame.display.set_caption("Bike Racing Game Refined")

# Player position
player_x, player_y = 400, 500
player_speed = 5

# Road parameters
```

```python
road_width = 400
road_color = (50, 50, 50)
road_rect = pygame.Rect(200, 0, road_width, window_size[1])

# Game loop
while True:
    for event in pygame.event.get():
        if event.type == pygame.QUIT:
            pygame.quit()
            sys.exit()

    # Handle player input
    keys = pygame.key.get_pressed()
    if keys[pygame.K_LEFT] and player_x > road_rect.left:
        player_x -= player_speed
    if keys[pygame.K_RIGHT] and player_x + 50 < road_rect.right:
        player_x += player_speed

    # Clear the screen
    screen.fill((255, 255, 255))

    # Draw the road
    pygame.draw.rect(screen, road_color, road_rect)

    # Draw the player
    pygame.draw.rect(screen, (0, 0, 255), (player_x, player_y,
    50, 50))

    # Update the display
    pygame.display.flip()
```

Add Graphics and Sound:

Enhance the visual appeal with graphics and add sound effects. Incorporate background music and bike engine sounds. To add sound effects follow the given code:

```python
# main.py (Add Sound Effects)

import pygame
import sys

# Initialize Pygame
pygame.init()

# Set up the game window
window_size = (800, 600)
screen = pygame.display.set_mode(window_size)
pygame.display.set_caption("Bike Racing Game")

# Load background image
background_image =
pygame.image.load("assets/images/background.png")

# Load bike sprite
bike_image = pygame.image.load("assets/images/bike.png")
bike_rect = bike_image.get_rect()

# Load sound effects
engine_sound = pygame.mixer.Sound("assets/sounds/engine.wav")
crash_sound = pygame.mixer.Sound("assets/sounds/crash.wav")

# Player position and speed
player_x, player_y = 400, 500
player_speed = 5

# Game state
score = 0

# Game loop
while True:
for event in pygame.event.get():
if event.type == pygame.QUIT:
pygame.quit()
sys.exit()

# Handle player input
```

```python
keys = pygame.key.get_pressed()
if keys[pygame.K_LEFT] and player_x > 0:
player_x -= player_speed
if keys[pygame.K_RIGHT] and player_x + 50 < window_size[0]:
player_x += player_speed

# Play engine sound when player moves
if keys[pygame.K_LEFT] or keys[pygame.K_RIGHT]:
engine_sound.play()
else:
engine_sound.stop()

# Update game logic
score += 1

# Clear the screen
screen.fill((255, 255, 255))

# Draw the background image
screen.blit(background_image, (0, 0))

# Draw the player (bike)
screen.blit(bike_image, (player_x, player_y))

# Display score
font = pygame.font.Font(None, 36)
score_text = font.render(f"Score: {score}", True, (0, 0, 0))
screen.blit(score_text, (10, 10))

# Update the display
pygame.display.flip()
```

Load and Display Bike Sprite:

Replace the basic blue rectangle representing the player with a bike sprite.

```python
pythonCopy code
# main.py (Add Bike Sprite)
```

```python
import pygame
import sys

# Initialize Pygame
pygame.init()

# Set up the game window
window_size = (800, 600)
screen = pygame.display.set_mode(window_size)
pygame.display.set_caption("Bike Racing Game")

# Load background image
background_image =
pygame.image.load("assets/images/background.png")

# Load bike sprite
bike_image = pygame.image.load("assets/images/bike.png")
bike_rect = bike_image.get_rect()

# Player position and speed
player_x, player_y = 400, 500
player_speed = 5

# Game state
score = 0

# Game loop
while True:
    for event in pygame.event.get():
        if event.type == pygame.QUIT:
            pygame.quit()
            sys.exit()

    # Handle player input
    keys = pygame.key.get_pressed()
    if keys[pygame.K_LEFT] and player_x > 0:
        player_x -= player_speed
    if keys[pygame.K_RIGHT] and player_x + 50 < window_size[0]:
        player_x += player_speed
```

```python
    # Update game logic
    score += 1

    # Clear the screen
    screen.fill((255, 255, 255))

    # Draw the background image
    screen.blit(background_image, (0, 0))

    # Draw the player (bike)
    screen.blit(bike_image, (player_x, player_y))

    # Display score
    font = pygame.font.Font(None, 36)
    score_text = font.render(f"Score: {score}", True, (0, 0, 0))
    screen.blit(score_text, (10, 10))

    # Update the display
    pygame.display.flip()
```

Implement Game Logic:

Expand the game logic to include scoring, obstacles, and win/lose conditions.

```python
# main.py (Game Logic)

import pygame
import sys

# Initialize Pygame
pygame.init()

# Set up the game window
window_size = (800, 600)
screen = pygame.display.set_mode(window_size)
pygame.display.set_caption("Bike Racing Game")

# Player position and speed
```

```python
player_x, player_y = 400, 500
player_speed = 5

# Road parameters
road_width = 400
road_color = (50, 50, 50)
road_rect = pygame.Rect(200, 0, road_width, window_size[1])

# Game state
score = 0

# Game loop
while True:
    for event in pygame.event.get():
        if event.type == pygame.QUIT:
            pygame.quit()
            sys.exit()

    # Handle player input
    keys = pygame.key.get_pressed()
    if keys[pygame.K_LEFT] and player_x > road_rect.left:
        player_x -= player_speed
    if keys[pygame.K_RIGHT] and player_x + 50 < road_rect.right:
        player_x += player_speed

    # Update game logic
    score += 1

    # Clear the screen
    screen.fill((255, 255, 255))

    # Draw the road
    pygame.draw.rect(screen, road_color, road_rect)

    # Draw the player
    pygame.draw.rect(screen, (0, 0, 255), (player_x, player_y,
    50, 50))

    # Display score
    font = pygame.font.Font(None, 36)
```

```python
    score_text = font.render(f"Score: {score}", True, (0, 0, 0))
    screen.blit(score_text, (10, 10))

    # Update the display
    pygame.display.flip()
```

Polish and Optimize:

Optimize your code, address any bugs, and add polish to improve the user experience. Implement smooth transitions and handle edge cases.

Test and Gather Feedback:

Thoroughly test your game to identify and fix any issues. Gather feedback from play testing to understand player interactions.

Document and Share:

Document your code, create a README file, and share your bike racing game project with others. Encourage collaboration and feedback.

You may take your bike racing game project from a rough prototype to a polished and completely working finished product by following these steps. You get better at creating a captivating and entertaining gaming experience with each iteration.

Simple racing game

Here is a sample bike racing code with 2 players. They start from same sport then compete to get to a specific point. Feel free to alter the code as you wish.

```python
import pygame
import random

# Initialize the game
pygame.init()

# Set up the game window
window_width = 800
window_height = 600
window = pygame.display.set_mode((window_width, window_height))
pygame.display.set_caption("Bike Competition Game")

# Set up the colors
white = (255, 255, 255)
black = (0, 0, 0)
red = (255, 0, 0)

# Set up the player and enemy variables
player_width = 50
player_height = 100
player_x = window_width // 4 - player_width // 2
player_y = window_height - player_height - 10
player_speed = 5

enemy_width = 50
enemy_height = 100
enemy_x = window_width * 3 // 4 - enemy_width // 2
enemy_y = window_height - enemy_height - 10
enemy_speed = 3

finish_line = window_height // 2

# Set up the game timer
game_time = pygame.time.get_ticks()
game_duration = 60000  # 1 minute in milliseconds

# Run the game loop
running = True
clock = pygame.time.Clock()
```

```python
while running:
    for event in pygame.event.get():
        if event.type == pygame.QUIT:
            running = False

    # Check if the game time has reached the duration
    current_time = pygame.time.get_ticks()
    if current_time - game_time >= game_duration:
        running = False

    # Move the player controlled by the user
    keys = pygame.key.get_pressed()
    if keys[pygame.K_UP] and player_y > 0:
        player_y -= player_speed

    # Move the player controlled by the system
    if enemy_y > 0:
        enemy_y -= enemy_speed

    # Check for collision with the finish line
    if player_y <= finish_line or enemy_y <= finish_line:
        running = False

    # Draw the game objects
    window.fill(white)
    pygame.draw.rect(window, black, (player_x, player_y,
    player_width, player_height))
    pygame.draw.rect(window, red, (enemy_x, enemy_y, enemy_width,
    enemy_height))
    pygame.draw.line(window, black, (0, finish_line),
    (window_width, finish_line))

    # Update the display
    pygame.display.update()
    clock.tick(60)

# Game over
pygame.quit()
```

Two rectangular bars, which depict bikes, are the result of the code shown above. The person operates one, while the system operates the other. As seen in the picture below, they compete to see who can hit the line at the center first.

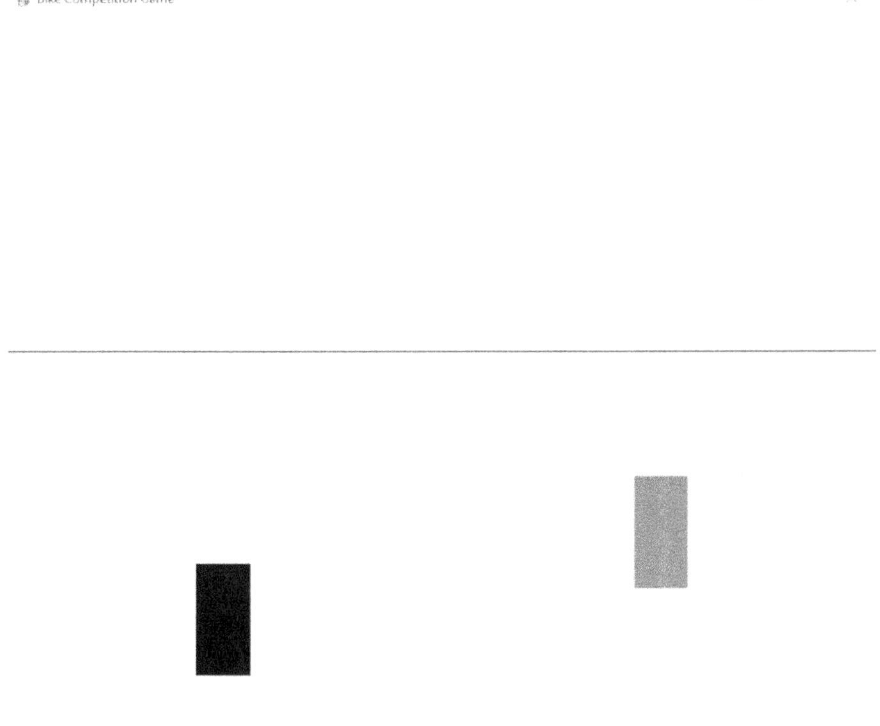

Testing and Debugging Strategies

Importance of Testing in Game Development

The success and quality of your Python game projects are greatly influenced by testing, which is an essential component of game development. Thorough testing guarantees that your games are pleasant and seamless for players, in addition to being functional. In this section, we'll examine the value of testing in the creation of video games and provide examples of several Python testing techniques.

Ensuring Game Functionality:

Make sure your game's core features are operating as intended before tackling more complex features and optimizations. Unit tests that are automated can aid in the validation of particular parts and operations.

```python
# test_game_functionality.py

import unittest
from game_module import Game

class TestGameFunctionality(unittest.TestCase):

    def test_initialization(self):
        game = Game()
```

```python
        self.assertIsNotNone(game, "Game object not created")

    def test_player_movement(self):
        game = Game()
        initial_x = game.player_x
        game.handle_input("right")
        self.assertNotEqual(game.player_x, initial_x, "Player not
        moving right")
```

Checking Collision Detection:

Collision detection is a critical aspect of many games, especially those involving player interaction with the environment. Testing ensures that collisions are accurately detected.

```python
# test_collision_detection.py

import unittest
from game_module import Game

class TestCollisionDetection(unittest.TestCase):

    def test_player_collision_with_obstacle(self):
        game = Game()
        game.player_x = 100
        game.obstacle_x = 100
        self.assertTrue(game.check_collision(), "Collision not
        detected")
```

Performance Testing:

Optimizing your game for performance is crucial, especially for resource-intensive games. Performance tests help identify bottlenecks and areas for improvement.

```python
# test_performance.py

import unittest
import time
from game_module import Game

class TestPerformance(unittest.TestCase):

    def test_game_performance(self):
        start_time = time.time()
        game = Game()
        # Simulate game loop for a certain duration
        for _ in range(1000):
            game.update()
        elapsed_time = time.time() - start_time
        self.assertTrue(elapsed_time < 1.0, "Game loop took too
        long")
```

User Interface (UI) Testing:

For games with graphical user interfaces, UI testing ensures that the visual elements and user interactions are responsive and aesthetically pleasing.

```python
# test_ui.py

import unittest
import pygame
from game_module import Game

class TestUITesting(unittest.TestCase):

    def test_ui_elements_visibility(self):
        pygame.init()
        game = Game()
        game.show_menu()
        self.assertTrue(game.menu_visible, "Menu not visible")
```

Integration Testing:

Integration tests evaluate the interactions between different components, ensuring that they work harmoniously together.

```python
# test_integration.py

import unittest
from game_module import Game

class TestIntegration(unittest.TestCase):

    def test_game_start_to_finish(self):
        game = Game()
        game.start()
        self.assertTrue(game.is_running, "Game not started")
        # Simulate gameplay
        for _ in range(100):
            game.update()
        game.end()
        self.assertFalse(game.is_running, "Game not ended")
```

Continuous Integration (CI) and Automated Testing:

Use continuous integration (CI) platforms like in Jenkins or GitHub Actions to incorporate testing into your development workflow. By ensuring that your game is regularly validated, automated testing helps to prevent the introduction of new issues.

.github/workflows/tests.yml

```yaml
name: Run Tests

on:
  push:
    branches:
      - main
```

```
jobs:
  test:
    runs-on: ubuntu-latest

    steps:
      - name: Checkout Repository
        uses: actions/checkout@v2

      - name: Set up Python
        uses: actions/setup-python@v2
        with:
          python-version: 3.8

      - name: Install Dependencies
        run: |
          pip install -r requirements.txt
      - name: Run Tests
        run: python -m unittest discover
```

The dependability of your Python games is greatly increased when thorough testing is incorporated into the process. Testing is essential to creating high-caliber games because it validates user interfaces, optimizes performance, and ensures fundamental functionality.

Debugging Techniques for Python Games

Debugging is an integral part of the game development process, helping identify and resolve issues that may arise during the creation of Python games. In this section, we'll explore effective debugging techniques tailored to the unique challenges of game development.

Print Statements:

Description: Utilize print statements to output variable values, messages, or checkpoints in your game code.

Code Example:

```python
def update_player_position():
    print(f"Current player position: ({player_x}, {player_y})")
    # Update player position logic
```

Logging:

Description: Implement a logging system to record important events and errors during runtime.

Code Example:

```python
import logging

logging.basicConfig(filename='game_log.txt', level=logging.DEBUG)

def game_start():
    logging.info('Game started')
```

Interactive Debugging with pdb:

Description: Use the Python Debugger (pdb) to interactively debug your code, set breakpoints, and inspect variables.

Code Example:

```python
import pdb

def complex_game_function():
    # Insert breakpoint
    pdb.set_trace()
    # Rest of the function logic
```

Visual Debugging with Pygame_sdl2:

Description: Pygame_sdl2 offers a visual debugging feature that allows you to draw shapes or images on the screen for debugging purposes.

Code Example:

```python
import pygame_sdl2 as pygame

def draw_debug_info():
    pygame.draw.rect(screen, (255, 0, 0), (debug_x, debug_y, 20,
    20))
```

Assertions:

Description: Use assert statements to enforce assumptions about the state of your program during development.

Code Example:

```python
def calculate_score(points):
    assert points >= 0, "Points should be non-negative"
    # Rest of the function logic
```

Code Profiling:

Description: Employ code profiling tools to identify performance bottlenecks and optimize your game.

Code Example (using cProfile):

```python
import cProfile

def profiled_function():
    # Function logic
```

```
cProfile.run('profiled_function()')
```

Exception Handling:

Description: Implement robust exception handling to gracefully manage errors and prevent crashes.

Code Example:

```
try:
    # Risky code
except Exception as e:
    print(f"An error occurred: {e}")
    # Handle the error gracefully
```

Visualizing Data with Matplotlib:

Description: Use Matplotlib to visualize data, such as the trajectory of game entities or statistical information.

Code Example:

```
import matplotlib.pyplot as plt

def plot_trajectory(x_values, y_values):
    plt.plot(x_values, y_values)
    plt.show()
```

Remote Debugging:

Description: Debug your game remotely using tools like PyCharm's remote debugging feature for more complex scenarios.

Setup:

- Install PyCharm on your development machine and on the machine running the game.
- Set up a remote debugger configuration in PyCharm.
- Run the PyCharm remote debugger server on the game machine.
- Connect your development machine's PyCharm to the remote debugger server.

With the help of these debugging approaches, you may find and fix problems in your Python game projects more efficiently. Every technique—from straightforward print statements to sophisticated visual debugging—offers a different viewpoint on the behavior of your game, improving the effectiveness and scope of the debugging process.

Iterative Testing and Improvement

A key component of Python game development is iterative testing and improvement, which guarantees that your games progress, get better, and give players an enjoyable experience. The concepts of iterative testing and improvement will be covered in this section, with a focus on the cycle of testing, evaluating, and improving your game.

Establishing a Testing Framework:

Description: Define a robust testing framework that includes unit tests, integration tests, performance tests, and UI tests. This framework forms the foundation for iterative testing.

Code Example (Using unittest):

```python
import unittest

class TestGameFunctionality(unittest.TestCase):
    def test_initialization(self):
```

```
    # Test game initialization logic
# More test methods...
```

Continuous Integration (CI) Integration:

Description: Integrate your testing framework into a CI system (e.g., Jenkins, GitHub Actions) to automate testing on code commits. This ensures that tests are run consistently throughout the development process.

Setup (GitHub Actions):

Create a **.github/workflows/tests.yml** file with configuration to run tests on each push.

Player Feedback and Playtesting:

Description: Gather feedback from players or beta testers to understand their experience. Analyze player behavior, identify pain points, and use this feedback to iterate on your game.

Feedback Form:

- Create a feedback form for players to provide structured feedback.
- Include questions about gameplay, controls, bugs encountered, and suggestions for improvement.

Performance Monitoring:

Description: Implement performance monitoring tools to collect data on your game's performance in real-world scenarios. Analyze the data to identify bottlenecks and areas for optimization.

Code Example (Using cProfile):

```
import cProfile

def profiled_function():
    # Function logic

cProfile.run('profiled_function()')
```

A/B Testing:

Description: By adding variations to your game and tracking player response, you may perform A/B testing. This lets you assess whether features or design decisions are more appealing to players by comparing them.

Implementation:

- Create two versions of a feature (A and B).
- Randomly assign players to either group and measure their engagement.

Iterative Gameplay Design:

Description: Iteratively design and implement gameplay mechanics. Regularly playtest these mechanics to ensure they contribute positively to the overall gaming experience.

Example:

- Iteratively refine the controls, adjusting sensitivity based on player feedback.
- Experiment with different enemy behaviors and gather player reactions.

Bug Tracking and Resolution:

Description: Maintain a system for tracking bugs and issues. Regularly review and prioritize these issues, addressing them in each development iteration.

Bug Tracking Tools:

- Use tools like Jira, Trello, or GitHub Issues to manage and prioritize bugs.

User Interface (UI) Refinement:

Description: Continuously refine the user interface based on usability testing and player feedback. Ensure that the UI is intuitive and enhances the overall gaming experience.

Iterative Refinement:

- Adjust button placements based on player interaction heatmaps.
- Test different color schemes for improved visibility.

Data-Driven Decision Making:

Description: Use analytics tools to gather data on player behavior. Analyze this data to make informed decisions about game design, feature implementation, and optimization.

Analytics Tools:

- Integrate tools like Google Analytics or custom analytics solutions into your game.

Documentation and Knowledge Sharing:

Description: Document lessons learned, insights, and improvements made during each iteration. Share this knowledge with the development team to foster continuous learning.

Documentation Tips:

- Maintain a development wiki with insights from playtests and testing outcomes.
- Conduct regular knowledge-sharing sessions.

You may establish a dynamic development cycle that stimulates creativity and guarantees the continuous progress of your Python games by adopting iterative testing and improvement. You get better at creating a polished, interesting, and fun gaming experience for your players with each iteration.

Optimizing Code for Performance

Profiling Your Python Code

To optimize Python game code and ensure peak performance, profiling is essential. We'll look at methods and resources for profiling your Python game code in this chapter.

Comprehending Profiling: In game development, profiling is essential since it measures execution time to pinpoint regions that require optimization.

Using the cProfile Module: Deterministic profiling of function execution time is possible with Python's cProfile module.

Code Example:

```python
import cProfile

def your_game_function():
    # Game logic

cProfile.run('your_game_function()')
```

Analyzing **cProfile** Output: Review the detailed report to identify functions consuming significant time.

Profiling Specific Sections: Profile specific sections to focus on critical areas.

Code Example:

```python
import cProfile

def critical_game_section():
    # Critical game logic

cProfile.run('critical_game_section()')
```

Using **timeit** for Microbenchmarking: Measure time for small code snippets using **timeit**.

Code Example:

```python
import timeit

def time_critical_operation():
    # Critical operation to optimize

elapsed_time = timeit.timeit(time_critical_operation, number=1000)
print(f"Time taken: {elapsed_time} seconds")
```

Memory Profiling with **memory_profiler**: **memory_profiler** tracks memory usage over time, essential for resource-intensive games.

Installation:

```
pip install memory-profiler
```

Code Example:

```python
from memory_profiler import profile

@profile
def memory_intensive_function():
    # Memory-intensive logic
```

Visual Profiling with **snakeviz**: **snakeviz** provides an interactive web-based visualization of **cProfile** results.

Installation:

```
pip install snakeviz
```

Usage:

```
python -m cProfile -o profile_data your_game_script.py
snakeviz profile_data
```

Identifying Hotspots and Optimizing: Focus on optimizing identified hotspots through algorithmic improvements or data structure optimizations.

Reprofiling After Optimization: After changes, re-run the profiler to ensure positive impacts on performance.

Code Example (Reprofiling):

```python
import cProfile

def optimized_game_function():
    # Optimized game logic

cProfile.run('optimized_game_function()')
```

Documentation and Best Practices: Document your profiling process, optimizations, and share best practices with your team for collective understanding.

By integrating profiling techniques, you systematically enhance Python game performance, providing players with a responsive and optimized gaming experience.

Implementing Optimization Strategies

For a gaming experience that is responsive and fluid, you must optimize your Python game code. This section will cover efficient optimization tactics and offer code examples to put them into practice.

Prior to beginning any improvements, utilize tools for performance profiling, such as cProfile, to locate any bottlenecks.

Code Example:

```python
import cProfile

def your_game_function():
    # Game logic

cProfile.run('your_game_function()')
```

Choose Efficient Data Structures: Select data structures that offer optimal performance for specific operations in your game.

Code Example:

```python
# Using a set for fast membership tests
unique_elements = {1, 2, 3, 4, 5}

# Using a deque for efficient appending and popping
```

```
from collections import deque
fifo_queue = deque()
fifo_queue.append(1)
item = fifo_queue.popleft()
```

Optimize Loops: Streamline loops by minimizing unnecessary operations and leveraging Python's built-in functions.

Code Example:

```
# Inefficient loop
result = []
for element in some_list:
    result.append(element * 2)

# Optimized using list comprehension
result = [element * 2 for element in some_list]
```

Utilize NumPy for Numeric Operations: For games with heavy numeric computations, NumPy provides optimized array operations.

Code Example:

```
import numpy as np

# Inefficient element-wise addition
result = [a + b for a, b in zip(array_a, array_b)]

# Optimized using NumPy
result = np.array(array_a) + np.array(array_b)
```

Cache Expensive Computations: Avoid redundant calculations by caching results when possible.

Code Example:

```python
# Without caching
result = expensive_function(data)
result_again = expensive_function(data)  # Recalculating

# With caching
if 'result' not in globals():
    result = expensive_function(data)
result_again = result  # Reusing cached result
```

Use Generators for Memory Efficiency: Generators produce values one at a time, reducing memory overhead.

Code Example:

```python
# List comprehension (creates entire list in memory)
squares = [x**2 for x in range(10)]

# Generator expression (produces values on-the-fly)
squares_generator = (x**2 for x in range(10))
```

Consider Just-In-Time (JIT) Compilation: Tools like Numba or PyPy use JIT compilation for performance improvements.

Code Example (Numba):

```python
from numba import jit

@jit(nopython=True)
def numba_optimized_function(data):
    # Numba-optimized logic
```

Minimize Global Variables: Reduce the use of global variables to enhance code readability and performance.

Code Example:

```python
# Global variable
global_variable = 10

# Function using global variable
def use_global_variable():
    return global_variable
```

These optimization strategies, when applied judiciously, can significantly enhance the performance of your Python game. Remember to profile your code before and after optimizations to measure the impact accurately.

Best Practices for Efficient Game Development

Developing games with Python should be optimized by following best practices that increase maintainability and efficiency. We'll examine important techniques and offer pertinent code samples for effective game creation in this section.

Use Descriptive Variable Names:

```python
# Poor naming
a = 10

# Improved naming
initial_player_health = 100
```

Leverage Functions for Modularity:

```python
# Non-modular code
player_x = player_x + 5
player_y = player_y + 2

# Modular code
def move_player(x_increment, y_increment):
```

```
    global player_x, player_y
    player_x += x_increment
    player_y += y_increment

move_player(5, 2)
```

Apply Object-Oriented Principles:

```
# Procedural approach
player_x = 0
player_y = 0

# Object-oriented approach
class Player:
    def __init__(self, x, y):
        self.x = x
        self.y = y

player = Player(0, 0)
```

Efficient Data Storage:

```
# Using a list for a small fixed-size array
coordinates = [0, 0]

# Using a tuple for immutable data
coordinates = (0, 0)

# Using a class for complex data
class Point:
    def __init__(self, x, y):
        self.x = x
        self.y = y

player_position = Point(0, 0)
```

Avoid Global Variables:

```python
# Using a global variable
global_variable = 10

# Passing parameters to functions
def use_global_variable(value):
    return value

result = use_global_variable(global_variable)
```

Optimize Loops:

```python
# Inefficient loop
result = []
for element in some_list:
    result.append(element * 2)

# Optimized using list comprehension
result = [element * 2 for element in some_list]
```

Handle Exceptions Appropriately:

```python
# Poor exception handling
try:
    result = 10 / 0
except:
    result = 0

# Improved exception handling
try:
    result = 10 / 0
except ZeroDivisionError:
    result = 0
```

Utilize NumPy for Numeric Operations:

```python
import numpy as np

# Inefficient element-wise addition
result = [a + b for a, b in zip(array_a, array_b)]

# Optimized using NumPy
result = np.array(array_a) + np.array(array_b)
```

Document Your Code:

```python
# Lack of documentation
def calculate_damage(player_attack, enemy_defense):
    return player_attack - enemy_defense

# Adding documentation
def calculate_damage(player_attack, enemy_defense):
    """

    Calculate the damage inflicted by a player based on their attack
    and the enemy's defense.

    Parameters:
    - player_attack (int): The attack power of the player.
    - enemy_defense (int): The defense strength of the enemy.

    Returns:
    int: The calculated damage.
    """

    return player_attack - enemy_defense
```

By incorporating these best practices, you'll create efficient, readable, and maintainable Python game code, ultimately enhancing the overall development process and player experience.

Advanced Game Mechanics

Building on Basic Concepts

Building upon fundamental ideas, you may develop intricate and captivating Python games. We'll look at how to expand your knowledge of game development into complex game mechanics in this chapter. Examples of pertinent code are given to show how these ideas can be used.

Implementing Advanced Player Controls:

Developing and integrating intricate and sophisticated control methods for players in a game or interactive program is known as "implementing advanced player controls."

Developers can provide players improved capabilities and interactions through the use of sophisticated player controls, making the game more immersive and captivating.

Code Example:

```python
# Basic player movement
def move_player(direction):
```

```python
    if direction == "up":
        player_y -= 1
    elif direction == "down":
        player_y += 1
    elif direction == "left":
        player_x -= 1
    elif direction == "right":
        player_x += 1


# Advanced player controls with acceleration
class Player:
    def __init__(self, x, y):
        self.x = x
        self.y = y
        self.speed = 1
        self.velocity_x = 0
        self.velocity_y = 0


    def move(self, direction):
        if direction == "up":
            self.velocity_y -= self.speed
        elif direction == "down":
            self.velocity_y += self.speed
        elif direction == "left":
            self.velocity_x -= self.speed
        elif direction == "right":
            self.velocity_x += self.speed


    def update_position(self):
        self.x += self.velocity_x
        self.y += self.velocity_y
```

Introducing Advanced Enemy AI:

Using Advanced Enemy AI has become important in modern game production to increase player interest. Sophisticated decision-making algorithms, sensory perception systems, and adaptive learning strategies are all employed in this evolution.

Randomness is introduced into decision-making and optimization is used to overcome the problems of computing complexity and predictability. In order to incorporate cooperative AI behavior for strategic gameplay and carefully balance difficulty levels, Advanced Enemy AI must be incorporated into game design. AI performance is improved by user input methods combined with simulated environment testing and iteration.

In order to guarantee that Advanced Enemy AI meets player expectations while providing a demanding and entertaining gaming experience, user experience considerations place a strong emphasis on intuitive behavior and customizable possibilities. To sum up, the introduction of Advanced Enemy AI is a noteworthy advancement in contemporary game development, enhancing the entire immersive experience of video games.

Code Example:

```python
# Basic enemy movement towards the player
def move_towards_player(player_x, player_y, enemy_x, enemy_y):
    if player_x > enemy_x:
        enemy_x += 1
    elif player_x < enemy_x:
        enemy_x -= 1

    if player_y > enemy_y:
        enemy_y += 1
    elif player_y < enemy_y:
        enemy_y -= 1

# Advanced enemy AI with predictive movement
class Enemy:
    def __init__(self, x, y, player):
        self.x = x
        self.y = y
        self.player = player

    def predict_player_movement(self):
```

```
if self.player.velocity_x > 0:
    self.x += 1
elif self.player.velocity_x < 0:
    self.x -= 1

if self.player.velocity_y > 0:
    self.y += 1
elif self.player.velocity_y < 0:
    self.y -= 1
```

Implementing Physics and Collisions:

A realistic and engaging gaming experience requires the effective application of collision and physics technologies. The use of physics engines—which replicate gravity and the rules of motion—is a crucial component that enables real-world item movement and interaction. In order to provide precise and visually cohesive interactions between game elements, collision detection algorithms are essential in determining when and how objects come into contact.

Code Example:

```
# Basic collision detection
def check_collision(player_x, player_y, obstacle_x, obstacle_y):
    if player_x == obstacle_x and player_y == obstacle_y:
        return True
    else:
        return False

# Advanced physics and collision with acceleration
class GameObject:
    def __init__(self, x, y):
        self.x = x
        self.y = y
        self.velocity_x = 0
        self.velocity_y = 0
```

```python
        self.acceleration_x = 0
        self.acceleration_y = 0

    def apply_force(self, force_x, force_y):
        self.acceleration_x += force_x
        self.acceleration_y += force_y

    def update_position(self):
        self.velocity_x += self.acceleration_x
        self.velocity_y += self.acceleration_y
        self.x += self.velocity_x
        self.y += self.velocity_y
```

Integrating Advanced Graphics and Animation:

To create visually appealing and immersive gaming experiences, modern graphics and animation must be integrated. Using state-of-the-art tools and methods, this procedure produces realistic graphics and smooth animations that enthrall players. Using cutting-edge graphics rendering engines, like Unreal Engine or Unity's High Definition Render Pipeline (HDRP), is a crucial component of this integration since they offer the framework for creating realistic scenes with excellent lighting, shadows, and post-processing effects.

Physically-based rendering (PBR) is one technique used frequently in advanced graphics to replicate the way materials interact with light, producing more realistic and aesthetically pleasing surfaces. The overall visual integrity of the game is improved by dynamic lighting algorithms and real-time global illumination, which help to create realistic and dynamic scenes.

Code Example:

```python
 # Basic graphics rendering
 def render_player(player_x, player_y):
     # Code to render the player at coordinates (player_x,
     player_y)
```

```python
# Advanced graphics with Pygame
import pygame

class Player:
    def __init__(self, x, y):
        self.x = x
        self.y = y
        self.image = pygame.image.load("player.png")

    def render(self, screen):
        screen.blit(self.image, (self.x, self.y))
```

Incorporating Multiplayer and Networking:

Including networking and multiplayer functionality is essential for making games that are entertaining and socially engaging. This procedure entails putting in place reliable technologies to enable player-to-player communication in real time, synchronize game states across various devices, and guarantee a smooth multiplayer experience. The effective integration of multiplayer and networking capabilities in contemporary games is facilitated by a number of important factors.

Code Example:

```python
# Basic multiplayer using sockets
# Server code
import socket

server = socket.socket(socket.AF_INET, socket.SOCK_STREAM)
server.bind(('localhost', 12345))
server.listen()

while True:
    client, address = server.accept()
    data = client.recv(1024)
```

```
    print(f"Received data: {data}")
    client.close()

 # Client code
 import socket

 client = socket.socket(socket.AF_INET, socket.SOCK_STREAM)
 client.connect(('localhost', 12345))
 client.send(b"Hello, server!")
 client.close()
```

Including complex mechanics is a necessary step in developing your Python game programming abilities. Building upon fundamental ideas will allow you to make captivating, feature-rich games that draw in players. These examples show how basic game development can lead to more complex and interesting experiences.

Implementing Complex Game Logic

Python game programming gains depth and intricacy from complex game logic. We'll look at how complex game mechanics can be used to provide engaging gameplay in this part. Useful code examples are given to show how these ideas may be applied.

Designing a Quest System:

A well-designed quest system gives players clear goals, significant advancement, and a feeling of direction in the virtual world. A quest system's effective design is influenced by a number of important factors.

Code Example:

```python
class Quest:
    def __init__(self, name, description, reward):
        self.name = name
        self.description = description
        self.reward = reward
        self.completed = False


class Player:
    def __init__(self, name):
        self.name = name
        self.quests = []

    def accept_quest(self, quest):
        self.quests.append(quest)

    def complete_quest(self, quest):
        quest.completed = True
        self.quests.remove(quest)
        # Grant the player the quest reward
        self.receive_reward(quest.reward)

    def receive_reward(self, reward):
        # Code to grant the player the specified reward
        pass
```

Implementing a Day-Night Cycle:

Including time management features, atmospheric effects, and dynamic lighting systems is necessary to implement an engaging day-night cycle in a game. Developers can create realistic day-to-night transitions by using atmospheric scattering, a dynamic skybox, and a directional light source for the sun. Precise control over the cycle is made possible by an adjustable time speed in conjunction with a robust time of day system. The immersive experience is enhanced by variations in surrounding features, color grading, and ambient lighting. A smooth and visually stunning gaming environment is also ensured by permitting user interaction with light sources and implementing performance optimization techniques, which raises player engagement and overall realism.

Code Example:

```python
class GameWorld:
    def __init__(self):
        self.time_of_day = 0  # 0 represents midnight

    def advance_time(self, hours):
        self.time_of_day = (self.time_of_day + hours) % 24

    def is_night(self):
        return 6 <= self.time_of_day <= 18

# Example usage
world = GameWorld()
world.advance_time(10)  # Advance time by 10 hours
if world.is_night():
    print("It's nighttime in the game world.")
```

Creating an Inventory System:

Implementing a structured framework that blends in seamlessly with gameplay is essential to designing an efficient inventory system in game development. The administration, storing, and handling of in-game things are all included in this system, necessitating the development of data structures for item representation, user interfaces for inventory display, and algorithms for item manipulation.

To maintain organizational efficiency, developers need to take into account things like item categorization, stacking, and sorting algorithms. Additionally, the player experience is improved with the incorporation of contextual actions, drag-and-drop functionality, and an intuitive UI. A strong and adaptable inventory system that fits with the game's mechanics and story and enhances the gameplay experience should take error handling, synchronization across multiplayer environments, and scalability for future expansions into account.

Code Example:

```python
class InventoryItem:
    def __init__(self, name, description, weight):
        self.name = name
        self.description = description
        self.weight = weight

class Inventory:
    def __init__(self):
        self.items = []

    def add_item(self, item):
        self.items.append(item)

    def remove_item(self, item):
        self.items.remove(item)

    def calculate_total_weight(self):
        return sum(item.weight for item in self.items)

# Example usage
player_inventory = Inventory()
sword = InventoryItem("Sword", "A sharp blade", 5)
player_inventory.add_item(sword)
total_weight = player_inventory.calculate_total_weight()
```

Implementing Dynamic NPC Behavior:

In game programming, dynamic NPC behavior entails building a complex system that enables non-player characters (NPCs) to behave in a realistic and responsive manner. Advanced decision-making techniques, like behavior trees or machine learning, must be integrated into this process in order for NPCs to be able to adjust to shifting player interactions and game conditions.

To replicate genuine responses, developers need to take into account elements such as goal-oriented behaviors, social interactions, and environmental awareness. A rich and immersive game experience is further enhanced by the incorporation of dynamic events, a variety of personalities, and the capacity for NPCs to change and grow over time. In order to guarantee that the dynamic NPC behavior system improves overall gameplay and offers players a dynamic and unpredictable virtual world to explore, it is imperative to strike a balance between complexity and performance optimization.

Code Example:

```python
import random

class NPC:
    def __init__(self, name):
        self.name = name

    def decide_action(self):
        actions = ["Attack", "Flee", "Trade", "Idle"]
        return random.choice(actions)

# Example usage
npc = NPC("Villager")
action = npc.decide_action()
print(f"{npc.name} decides to {action}.")
```

Creating a Crafting System:

In game development, crafting systems refer to the process of creating a complete structure that allows users to craft, alter, and improve in-game objects, which increases player interaction and advancement. The creation of item recipes, resource collection mechanisms, and crafting interfaces are all part of this complex system. It is imperative for makers of video games to create a logical arrangement of components, instruments, and schematics that allows players to explore and uncover novel crafting opportunities.

The player experience is improved by including an easy-to-use UI, simple crafting mechanics, and feedback systems. A well-rounded and engaging crafting system is also influenced by factors like skill advancement, rarity levels, and the incorporation of crafting into the game's story. Maintaining equilibrium between ease of use and complexity guarantees that the crafting system complements the entire layout of the game, encouraging ingenuity and giving players a significant path to success and customization.

Code Example:

```python
class CraftingRecipe:
    def __init__(self, name, ingredients, result):
        self.name = name
        self.ingredients = ingredients
        self.result = result


class CraftingSystem:
    def __init__(self):
        self.recipes = []


    def craft_item(self, recipe):
        if all(item in player_inventory.items for item in
        recipe.ingredients):
            for item in recipe.ingredients:
                player_inventory.remove_item(item)
            player_inventory.add_item(recipe.result)
            return True
        else:
            return False

# Example usage
crafting_system = CraftingSystem()
sword_recipe = CraftingRecipe("Sword", ["Iron Ingot", "Wood"],
"Iron Sword")
crafting_system.recipes.append(sword_recipe)
crafting_success = crafting_system.craft_item(sword_recipe)
```

These illustrations explain how intricate game logic is implemented, including crafting systems and dynamic NPC behavior. You may design complex games with intricate systems that captivate and challenge players, giving them a rich and immersive gaming experience, by including these mechanics.

Integrating Advanced Input Systems

Developing complex games in Python requires optimizing player interactions via sophisticated input methods. We'll look at how to use sophisticated input methods to make games more responsive and immersive in this section. Useful code examples are given to show how these ideas may be applied.

Implementing Mouse Input:

When using mouse input in game development, one must design a flexible, responsive system that accurately interprets user input. Mouse input is used by developers for a variety of tasks, such as dragging, clicking, and pointing, which allow users to interact with in-game objects and navigate the game world.

This procedure includes cursor tracking, effective event processing, and mouse device consideration. The user experience is improved by implementing feedback methods, such as visual cues or modifications to the cursor's look. A smooth and natural way of interaction, mouse input is essential to the design of user interfaces, camera controls, and other gameplay elements in many PC and browser-based games.

Code Example:

```python
import pygame

class Player:
    def __init__(self):
        self.x = 0
        self.y = 0
```

```python
    def move_towards_mouse(self):
        mouse_x, mouse_y = pygame.mouse.get_pos()
        angle = math.atan2(mouse_y - self.y, mouse_x - self.x)
        speed = 5
        self.x += speed * math.cos(angle)
        self.y += speed * math.sin(angle)

# Example usage
player = Player()
while running:
    for event in pygame.event.get():
        if event.type == pygame.QUIT:
            running = False
    player.move_towards_mouse()
```

Integrating Game Controllers:

The process of integrating game controllers into game development is extensive and aims to improve player experience by enabling smooth and responsive input. By using standardized input APIs, developers can integrate support for a variety of gaming controllers, including consoles, PC peripherals, and specialized devices. This entails establishing a logical and user-friendly control scheme by translating controller inputs to in-game activities.

Incorporating feedback methods like as sensations on the controller or visual signals can improve player immersion. Cross-platform compatibility is another factor that developers take into account to guarantee uniform controller support across various gaming systems. When game controllers are successfully integrated, gameplay is optimized and players are given a comfortable and adaptable input method, which enhances the immersion and enjoyment of the gaming experience.

Code Example:

```python
import pygame

class Player:
    def __init__(self):
        self.x = 0
        self.y = 0

    def move_with_controller(self):
        joystick_count = pygame.joystick.get_count()
        if joystick_count > 0:
            joystick = pygame.joystick.Joystick(0)
            joystick.init()
            speed = 5
            self.x += joystick.get_axis(0) * speed
            self.y += joystick.get_axis(1) * speed

# Example usage
player = Player()
while running:
    for event in pygame.event.get():
        if event.type == pygame.QUIT:
            running = False
    player.move_with_controller()
```

Implementing Touch Controls for Mobile Devices:

The process of integrating touch controllers for mobile devices into game development is complex and aims to produce a user interface that is responsive and easy to use. To convert user input into in-game actions, developers use touch gestures like swipes, taps, and multi-finger interactions. This entails putting responsive feedback methods, gesture detection algorithms, and touch event processing into practice.

It is necessary to carefully develop the user interface design to provide visibility, accessibility, and ease of use while taking into account the limits of touch screens. Additionally, for a consistent and entertaining mobile gaming experience, touch controls must be optimized for a range of screen sizes and orientations. Touch controls are a great way to improve player engagement since they offer a fluid and immersive interaction style that is specifically designed for mobile devices.

Code Example:

```python
import pygame

class Player:
    def __init__(self):
        self.x = 0
        self.y = 0

    def move_with_touch(self):
        for event in pygame.event.get():
            if event.type == pygame.FINGERDOWN:
                touch_x, touch_y = event.x, event.y
                # Process touch input and move the player
                accordingly

# Example usage
player = Player()
while running:
    for event in pygame.event.get():
        if event.type == pygame.QUIT:
            running = False
    player.move_with_touch()
```

Creating Custom Input Gestures:

Creating a specialized system that can understand and react to user input in ways other than the conventional keyboard and mouse interactions is required when designing bespoke input gestures for games. For touchscreens, motion controllers, and other input devices, developers can incorporate gesture recognition to enable players to carry out activities with natural and customized gestures.

To guarantee precise and responsive gesture identification, this procedure necessitates the integration of gesture libraries, exact tracking algorithms, and feedback mechanisms. Tailored input gestures improve gameplay by offering a more engaging and dynamic experience, supporting a wide variety of input devices, and enabling players to interact with the game in novel ways. The effectiveness of this system depends on striking a precise balance between guaranteeing usability and identifying distinctive gestures, which results in a dynamic and captivating user interface that adheres to the game's design concepts.

Code Example:

```python
import pygame

class Player:
    def __init__(self):
        self.x = 0
        self.y = 0

    def perform_custom_gesture(self):
        gesture = detect_custom_gesture()  # Implement gesture
        detection logic
        if gesture == "SwipeRight":
            self.x += 10
        elif gesture == "SwipeLeft":
            self.x -= 10
        # Handle other custom gestures

# Example usage
player = Player()
while running:
    for event in pygame.event.get():
        if event.type == pygame.QUIT:
            running = False
    player.perform_custom_gesture()
```

Utilizing Advanced Keyboard Input:

The utilization of sophisticated keyboard input in game development entails the establishment of an adaptable and scalable framework that amplifies player control and engagement. Key mapping and customisation, effective input handling, multi-key input and combo support, and key state tracking are among the features that developers value.

A more dynamic and effective player experience is enhanced by simultaneous input handling, key macros, and scripting; accessibility considerations and feedback mechanisms guarantee inclusivity. Advanced keyboard input is included in a way that complements the general game mechanics, giving players a responsive, immersive, and customized gaming experience that can be adjusted to suit different playstyles and tastes.

Code Example:

```python
import pygame

class Player:
    def __init__(self):
        self.x = 0
        self.y = 0
        self.speed = 5

    def handle_keyboard_input(self):
        keys = pygame.key.get_pressed()
        if keys[pygame.K_LEFT]:
            self.x -= self.speed
        elif keys[pygame.K_RIGHT]:
            self.x += self.speed
        if keys[pygame.K_UP]:
            self.y -= self.speed
        elif keys[pygame.K_DOWN]:
            self.y += self.speed

 # Example usage
 player = Player()
```

```
while running:
    for event in pygame.event.get():
        if event.type == pygame.QUIT:
            running = False
    player.handle_keyboard_input()
```

These cutting-edge input technologies can be integrated to give players a variety of ways to engage with your Python games. A more dynamic and captivating gaming experience is enhanced by the use of mouse input, game controllers, touch controls, bespoke gestures, and sophisticated keyboard input, among other technologies.

3D Game Programming with Python

Introduction to 3D Graphics

Python game programming gains more depth when it ventures into 3D visuals. This chapter will cover the fundamentals of 3D graphics, outlining ideas and offering pertinent code samples to get you started on the thrilling path of creating 3D games.

Setting Up a 3D Environment:

Setting up a 3D environment involves creating and configuring the necessary components to build a three-dimensional virtual space for use in a game, simulation, or other interactive applications.

Code Example:

```python
import pygame
from pygame.locals import *
from OpenGL.GL import *
from OpenGL.GLUT import *

# Initialize Pygame
pygame.init()
width, height = 800, 600
pygame.display.set_mode((width, height), DOUBLEBUF | OPENGL)
```

```python
pygame.display.set_caption("3D Graphics Introduction")

# Set up the perspective
glMatrixMode(GL_PROJECTION)
gluPerspective(45, (width / height), 0.1, 50.0)
glMatrixMode(GL_MODELVIEW)
gluLookAt(0, 0, -5, 0, 0, 0, 0, 1, 0)

# Game loop
while True:
    for event in pygame.event.get():
        if event.type == pygame.QUIT:
            pygame.quit()
            quit()

    # Clear the screen
    glClear(GL_COLOR_BUFFER_BIT | GL_DEPTH_BUFFER_BIT)

    # Draw a cube
    glutSolidCube(1)

    # Update the display
    pygame.display.flip()
    pygame.time.wait(10)
```

Creating 3D Objects:

Creating 3D objects involves designing and constructing three-dimensional models that can be used in various applications such as games, animations, simulations, or virtual reality experiences.

Code Example:

```python
def draw_cube():
    glBegin(GL_QUADS)
    vertices = [
        [1, -1, -1],
```

```python
        [1, 1, -1],
        [-1, 1, -1],
        [-1, -1, -1],
        [1, -1, 1],
        [1, 1, 1],
        [-1, -1, 1],
        [-1, 1, 1]
    ]
    edges = [
        [0, 1],
        [1, 2],
        [2, 3],
        [3, 0],
        [0, 4],
        [1, 5],
        [2, 6],
        [3, 7],
        [4, 5],
        [5, 6],
        [6, 7],
        [7, 4]
    ]
    for edge in edges:
        for vertex in edge:
            glVertex3fv(vertices[vertex])
    glEnd()

# Game loop
while True:
    for event in pygame.event.get():
        if event.type == pygame.QUIT:
            pygame.quit()
            quit()

    # Clear the screen
    glClear(GL_COLOR_BUFFER_BIT | GL_DEPTH_BUFFER_BIT)

    # Draw a customized 3D object (cube)
    draw_cube()
```

```
# Update the display
pygame.display.flip()
pygame.time.wait(10)
```

Implementing 3D Transformations:

Implementing 3D transformations involves applying various mathematical operations to manipulate the position, rotation, and scale of 3D objects in a virtual space.

Code Example:

```
angle = 0

# Game loop
while True:
    for event in pygame.event.get():
        if event.type == pygame.QUIT:
            pygame.quit()
            quit()

    # Clear the screen
    glClear(GL_COLOR_BUFFER_BIT | GL_DEPTH_BUFFER_BIT)

    # Apply 3D transformations (rotate the cube)
    glPushMatrix()
    glRotatef(angle, 1, 1, 1)
    draw_cube()
    glPopMatrix()

    # Update the display
    pygame.display.flip()
    pygame.time.wait(10)

    # Increment the rotation angle
    angle += 1
```

Adding 3D Lighting:

Adding 3D lighting involves incorporating light sources and configuring their properties to illuminate 3D objects in a virtual environment.

Code Example:

```python
# Enable lighting
glEnable(GL_LIGHTING)
glEnable(GL_LIGHT0)
light_position = (1, 1, 1, 0)
glLightfv(GL_LIGHT0, GL_POSITION, light_position)

# Game loop
while True:
    for event in pygame.event.get():
        if event.type == pygame.QUIT:
            pygame.quit()
            quit()

    # Clear the screen
    glClear(GL_COLOR_BUFFER_BIT | GL_DEPTH_BUFFER_BIT)

    # Apply 3D transformations (rotate the lit cube)
    glPushMatrix()
    glRotatef(angle, 1, 1, 1)
    draw_cube()
    glPopMatrix()

    # Update the display
    pygame.display.flip()
    pygame.time.wait(10)

    # Increment the rotation angle
    angle += 1
```

Creating games with 3D graphics opens you a world of possibilities for amazing visuals. These illustrations offer a fundamental comprehension of establishing a three-dimensional scene, creating objects, executing adjustments, and integrating illumination. These ideas will become the foundation for increasingly complex and engaging games as you learn more about developing 3D games.

Implementing 3D Game Mechanics

Your Python games will come to life and become interactive when you implement 3D game elements. This section will cover important ideas and offer pertinent code samples to help you create dynamic and engaging 3D gaming experiences.

Handling 3D Player Movement:

Handling 3D player movement involves managing the controls and mechanics that allow players to navigate and move within a three-dimensional virtual environment.

Code Example:

```
import pygame
from pygame.locals import *
from OpenGL.GL import *
from OpenGL.GLUT import *

class Player:
    def __init__(self):
        self.x, self.y, self.z = 0, 0, 0
        self.speed = 0.1

    def move_forward(self):
        self.z -= self.speed

# Game setup
pygame.init()
width, height = 800, 600
pygame.display.set_mode((width, height), DOUBLEBUF | OPENGL)
pygame.display.set_caption("3D Game Mechanics")
```

```python
glMatrixMode(GL_PROJECTION)
gluPerspective(45, (width / height), 0.1, 50.0)
glMatrixMode(GL_MODELVIEW)
gluLookAt(0, 0, 5, 0, 0, 0, 0, 1, 0)

player = Player()

# Game loop
while True:
    for event in pygame.event.get():
        if event.type == pygame.QUIT:
            pygame.quit()
            quit()

    keys = pygame.key.get_pressed()
    if keys[pygame.K_w]:
        player.move_forward()

    glClear(GL_COLOR_BUFFER_BIT | GL_DEPTH_BUFFER_BIT)
    glPushMatrix()
    glTranslatef(player.x, player.y, player.z)
    glutSolidCube(1)
    glPopMatrix()

    pygame.display.flip()
    pygame.time.wait(10)
```

Implementing 3D Collision Detection:

Implementing 3D collision detection involves incorporating algorithms and mechanisms to detect and respond to collisions between objects in a three-dimensional virtual environment.

Code Example:

```python
class GameObject:
    def __init__(self, x, y, z):
```

```python
        self.x, self.y, self.z = x, y, z
        self.width, self.height, self.depth = 1, 1, 1

    def check_collision(self, other_object):
        if (
            self.x < other_object.x + other_object.width and
            self.x + self.width > other_object.x and
            self.y < other_object.y + other_object.height and
            self.y + self.height > other_object.y and
            self.z < other_object.z + other_object.depth and
            self.z + self.depth > other_object.z
        ):
            return True
        return False


# Game setup and objects creation
player = Player()
obstacle = GameObject(0, 0, -5)


# Game loop
while True:
    for event in pygame.event.get():
        if event.type == pygame.QUIT:
            pygame.quit()
            quit()

    keys = pygame.key.get_pressed()
    if keys[pygame.K_w]:
        player.move_forward()

    # Check collision with the obstacle
    if player.check_collision(obstacle):
        print("Collision detected!")

    glClear(GL_COLOR_BUFFER_BIT | GL_DEPTH_BUFFER_BIT)
    glPushMatrix()
    glTranslatef(player.x, player.y, player.z)
    glutSolidCube(1)
    glPopMatrix()
```

```python
glPushMatrix()
glTranslatef(obstacle.x, obstacle.y, obstacle.z)
glutSolidCube(1)
glPopMatrix()

pygame.display.flip()
pygame.time.wait(10)
```

Implementing 3D Animation:

Implementing 3D animation involves creating and controlling the movement and behavior of three-dimensional objects in a virtual environment.

Code Example:

```python
class AnimatedObject:
    def __init__(self):
        self.angle = 0

    def animate(self):
        self.angle += 1

# Game setup and object creation
animated_object = AnimatedObject()

# Game loop
while True:
    for event in pygame.event.get():
        if event.type == pygame.QUIT:
            pygame.quit()
            quit()

    animated_object.animate()

    glClear(GL_COLOR_BUFFER_BIT | GL_DEPTH_BUFFER_BIT)
    glPushMatrix()
    glTranslatef(0, 0, -5)
    glRotatef(animated_object.angle, 1, 1, 1)
```

```python
    glutSolidCube(1)
    glPopMatrix()

    pygame.display.flip()
    pygame.time.wait(10)
```

Incorporating 3D Physics:

Incorporating 3D physics involves integrating realistic physical behaviors and interactions into a three-dimensional virtual environment.

Code Example:

```python
class PhysicsObject:
    def __init__(self, x, y, z, mass):
        self.x, self.y, self.z = x, y, z
        self.velocity_x, self.velocity_y, self.velocity_z = 0, 0,
        0
        self.mass = mass

    def apply_force(self, force_x, force_y, force_z):
        acceleration_x = force_x / self.mass
        acceleration_y = force_y / self.mass
        acceleration_z = force_z / self.mass
        self.velocity_x += acceleration_x
        self.velocity_y += acceleration_y
        self.velocity_z += acceleration_z

    def update_position(self):
        self.x += self.velocity_x
        self.y += self.velocity_y
        self.z += self.velocity_z

# Game setup and physics object creation
physics_object = PhysicsObject(0, 0, -5, 1)

# Game loop
```

```python
while True:
    for event in pygame.event.get():
        if event.type == pygame.QUIT:
            pygame.quit()
            quit()

    keys = pygame.key.get_pressed()
    if keys[pygame.K_w]:
        physics_object.apply_force(0, 0, -0.1)

    physics_object.update_position()

    glClear(GL_COLOR_BUFFER_BIT | GL_DEPTH_BUFFER_BIT)
    glPushMatrix()
    glTranslatef(physics_object.x, physics_object.y,
    physics_object.z)
    glutSolidCube(1)
    glPopMatrix()

    pygame.display.flip()
    pygame.time.wait(10)
```

Handling player movement, collision detection, animation, and physics are all part of implementing 3D game mechanics. The fundamental ideas shown in these examples will assist you in incorporating these dynamics into your Python 3D games. These ideas will provide the cornerstone for developing more complex and captivating gaming experiences.

Utilizing Popular 3D Libraries

Including well-known 3D libraries will greatly improve your Python game's functionality and development process. This section will examine how common 3D libraries are used, with pertinent code samples to show how they may be used to create complex and eye-catching games.

Using Pygame with PyOpenGL for 3D Rendering:

Using Pygame with PyOpenGL allows for the combination of Pygame's functionality with PyOpenGL's capabilities to enable 3D rendering in Python.

By using Pygame with PyOpenGL, developers can leverage Pygame's features for creating interactive 2D games and applications, while also accessing the power of PyOpenGL to render 3D graphics.

Code Example:

```python
import pygame
from pygame.locals import *
from OpenGL.GL import *
from OpenGL.GLUT import *

# Initialize Pygame
pygame.init()
width, height = 800, 600
pygame.display.set_mode((width, height), DOUBLEBUF | OPENGL)
pygame.display.set_caption("Using Pygame with PyOpenGL")

# Set up the perspective
glMatrixMode(GL_PROJECTION)
gluPerspective(45, (width / height), 0.1, 50.0)
glMatrixMode(GL_MODELVIEW)
gluLookAt(0, 0, 5, 0, 0, 0, 0, 1, 0)

# Game loop
while True:
    for event in pygame.event.get():
        if event.type == pygame.QUIT:
            pygame.quit()
            quit()

    # Clear the screen
    glClear(GL_COLOR_BUFFER_BIT | GL_DEPTH_BUFFER_BIT)

    # Draw a cube using PyOpenGL
    glutSolidCube(1)
```

```python
# Update the display
pygame.display.flip()
pygame.time.wait(10)
```

Utilizing Panda3D for Advanced 3D Game Development:

Utilizing Panda3D allows for advanced 3D game development, providing a powerful framework and toolset for creating immersive and interactive games.

Code Example:

```python
from direct.showbase.ShowBase import ShowBase
from direct.task import Task

class MyGame(ShowBase):
    def __init__(self):
        ShowBase.__init__(self)

        # Load a 3D model
        self.panda_model =
        self.loader.loadModel("models/panda-model")
        self.panda_model.reparentTo(self.render)
        self.panda_model.setScale(0.1, 0.1, 0.1)
        self.panda_model.setPos(0, 0, 0)

        # Set up the camera
        self.disableMouse()
        self.camera.setPos(0, -10, 0)

        # Schedule a task for animation
        self.taskMgr.add(self.animate_panda, "animate_panda_task")

    def animate_panda(self, task):
        # Rotate the panda model
        self.panda_model.setH(self.panda_model.getH() + 1.0)
```

```python
        return Task.cont

# Run the game
game = MyGame()
game.run()
```

Integrating Blender as a 3D Modeling Tool:

Integrating Blender as a 3D modeling tool allows for the seamless use of Blender's powerful features and capabilities within the context of a larger 3D development pipeline.

Code Example:

```python
# This code assumes you have Blender installed and the bpy module
is available
import bpy

# Create a new mesh
mesh = bpy.data.meshes.new(name="MyMesh")
obj = bpy.data.objects.new("MyObject", mesh)

# Link the object to the scene
bpy.context.scene.collection.objects.link(obj)

# Set mesh data
mesh.vertices.add(4)
mesh.vertices[0].co = (0, 0, 0)
mesh.vertices[1].co = (1, 0, 0)
mesh.vertices[2].co = (1, 1, 0)
mesh.vertices[3].co = (0, 1, 0)

mesh.faces.add(1)
mesh.faces[0].vertices = (0, 1, 2, 3)

# Update the mesh
mesh.update()
```

Using well-known 3D libraries like Blender, Panda3D, and Pygame with PyOpenGL might help you on your Python game development path. These libraries provide strong tools for modeling, rendering, and making eye-catching 3D games. You'll discover a wealth of materials and community assistance as you investigate these possibilities to help you achieve your game development objectives.

Networking and Multiplayer Games

Basics of Networking for Games

In order for players to communicate, connect, and share gaming experiences, networking is essential to the creation of multiplayer games. This chapter will cover the foundations of networking for Python games, with code examples to highlight important ideas.

Using Python's Socket Library for Basic Networking:

This involves utilizing the Socket module in Python to establish network connections and communicate between different devices.

Python's Socket module offers a collection of methods and classes that let programmers build network applications, like peer-to-peer connections and client-server communication. It makes data transmission and reception across multiple network protocols possible, including User Datagram Protocol (UDP) and TCP (Transmission Control Protocol).

Developers can implement fundamental networking functions, such as creating connections, transmitting and receiving data packets, and handling network faults, by using the Socket library. As a result, programs that can interact and share data with other networked devices can be developed.

The Socket package in Python offers a versatile and potent toolkit for creating simple networking applications. It makes network connection establishment easier and lets programmers add network features to Python applications.

Code Example:

```python
import socket
import threading

# Server-side code
def start_server():
    server_socket = socket.socket(socket.AF_INET,
    socket.SOCK_STREAM)
    server_socket.bind(('0.0.0.0', 5555))
    server_socket.listen()

    print("Server listening for incoming connections...")

    while True:
        client_socket, client_address = server_socket.accept()
        print(f"Accepted connection from {client_address}")

        # Handle the client in a separate thread
        client_handler = threading.Thread(target=handle_client,
        args=(client_socket,))
        client_handler.start()

def handle_client(client_socket):
    # Receive and send data
    request = client_socket.recv(1024).decode('utf-8')
    print(f"Received data from client: {request}")

    response = "Hello from the server!"
    client_socket.send(response.encode('utf-8'))

    client_socket.close()

# Client-side code
def start_client():
```

```python
    client_socket = socket.socket(socket.AF_INET,
    socket.SOCK_STREAM)
    client_socket.connect(('127.0.0.1', 5555))

    # Send and receive data
    message = "Hello from the client!"
    client_socket.send(message.encode('utf-8'))

    response = client_socket.recv(1024).decode('utf-8')
    print(f"Received response from server: {response}")

    client_socket.close()

# Run the server and client in separate threads
server_thread = threading.Thread(target=start_server)
client_thread = threading.Thread(target=start_client)

server_thread.start()
client_thread.start()
```

Using Python's socketserver Module for a Simple TCP Server:

Without needing to learn low-level socket programming, creating TCP servers is quick and easy with Python's socketserver module. A lot of the complexity is abstracted away, enabling developers to create and launch server apps more rapidly.

Developers can quickly construct a TCP server by subclassing the socketserver module and using it.TCPServer class and adding the required functionality to the matching handler class. The framework handles handling numerous connections at once, accepting incoming connections, and managing client requests.

Code Example:

```python
import socketserver

class MyTCPHandler(socketserver.BaseRequestHandler):
    def handle(self):
        # Receive and send data
        data = self.request.recv(1024).decode('utf-8')
        print(f"Received data from client: {data}")

        response = "Hello from the server!"
        self.request.sendall(response.encode('utf-8'))

# Create the server
server_address = ('0.0.0.0', 5555)
server = socketserver.TCPServer(server_address, MyTCPHandler)

print("Server listening for incoming connections...")
server.serve_forever()
```

Creating a Simple UDP Server and Client in Python:

The User Datagram Protocol (UDP) is used to establish communication between a server and client when creating a basic Python UDP server and client.

Data packets can be sent between devices using the connectionless UDP protocol without requiring a formal connection to be established. Applications that need for quick and effective data transmission frequently employ it.

Code Example:

```python
import socket

# Server-side code
server_socket = socket.socket(socket.AF_INET, socket.SOCK_DGRAM)
server_socket.bind(('0.0.0.0', 5555))
```

```python
print("Server listening for incoming connections...")

while True:
    data, client_address = server_socket.recvfrom(1024)
    print(f"Received data from client: {data.decode('utf-8')}")

    # Respond to the client
    response = "Hello from the server!"
    server_socket.sendto(response.encode('utf-8'), client_address)

# Client-side code
client_socket = socket.socket(socket.AF_INET, socket.SOCK_DGRAM)

# Send and receive data
message = "Hello from the client!"
client_socket.sendto(message.encode('utf-8'), ('127.0.0.1', 5555))

response, server_address = client_socket.recvfrom(1024)
print(f"Received response from server:
{response.decode('utf-8')}")

client_socket.close()
```

Gaining an understanding of Python networking fundamentals enables you to connect game clients and servers. Simple TCP and UDP server-client communication is demonstrated in the examples, which can be used as a basis for adding multiplayer features to your Python games. If you want to guarantee a satisfying multiplayer gaming experience, you might think about implementing more sophisticated networking theories and security protocols.

Implementing Multiplayer Functionality

Your Python games gain a dynamic and social element when you enable multiplayer capabilities. We'll examine how multiplayer features are implemented in this section, going over important ideas like synchronization and client-server communication. The above code samples show you how to create a simple multiplayer Python game.

Setting Up a Simple Multiplayer Server:

Setting up a simple multiplayer server involves configuring and deploying a server that allows multiple players to connect and interact with each other in a multiplayer game or application.

Code Example:

```python
import socket
import threading

# Server-side code
class MultiplayerServer:
    def __init__(self):
        self.server_socket = socket.socket(socket.AF_INET,
        socket.SOCK_STREAM)
        self.server_socket.bind(('0.0.0.0', 5555))
        self.server_socket.listen()

        self.clients = []
        print("Server listening for incoming connections...")

    def start(self):
        while True:
            client_socket, client_address =
            self.server_socket.accept()
            print(f"Accepted connection from {client_address}")

            # Add the new client to the list
            self.clients.append((client_socket, client_address))

            # Handle the client in a separate thread
            client_handler =
            threading.Thread(target=self.handle_client,
            args=(client_socket,))
            client_handler.start()
```

```python
    def handle_client(self, client_socket):
        while True:
            try:
                # Receive and broadcast data
                data = client_socket.recv(1024)
                if not data:
                    break

                message = data.decode('utf-8')
                print(f"Received message: {message}")

                # Broadcast the message to all clients
                self.broadcast(message, client_socket)
            except Exception as e:
                print(f"Error handling client: {e}")
                break

    def broadcast(self, message, sender_socket):
        for client, _ in self.clients:
            if client != sender_socket:
                try:
                    client.send(message.encode('utf-8'))
                except Exception as e:
                    print(f"Error broadcasting to a client: {e}")

# Run the server
server = MultiplayerServer()
server.start()
```

Creating a Multiplayer Game Client:

Creating a multiplayer game client involves developing the client-side code
that allows players to connect to a multiplayer game server and interact with
other players in real-time.

Code Example:

```python
import socket
import threading

# Client-side code
class MultiplayerClient:
    def __init__(self):
        self.client_socket = socket.socket(socket.AF_INET,
        socket.SOCK_STREAM)
        self.client_socket.connect(('127.0.0.1', 5555))

        # Start a separate thread for receiving messages
        receive_thread =
        threading.Thread(target=self.receive_messages)
        receive_thread.start()

    def receive_messages(self):
        while True:
            try:
                # Receive and display messages
                data = self.client_socket.recv(1024)
                if not data:
                    break

                message = data.decode('utf-8')
                print(f"Received message: {message}")
            except Exception as e:
                print(f"Error receiving messages: {e}")
                break

    def send_message(self, message):
        try:
            # Send the message to the server
            self.client_socket.send(message.encode('utf-8'))
        except Exception as e:
            print(f"Error sending message: {e}")

# Example usage
client = MultiplayerClient()
while True:
    user_input = input("Enter your message: ")
```

```
client.send_message(user_input)
```

The provided code showcases the basic structure for a simple multiplayer server and client in Python. This serves as a foundation for more complex implementations in your Python games. As you delve deeper into multiplayer game development, consider incorporating features like player synchronization, game state updates, and security measures to ensure a seamless and secure multiplayer gaming experience.

Addressing Challenges in Online Gaming

A new set of issues with performance, synchronization, and security arises with online gaming. In order to show how to overcome typical obstacles in Python game creation, we'll cover them in this part along with some sample code.

Mitigating Latency with Client-Side Prediction:

Adding methods to the client-side code of a networked application or game to reduce the negative effects of network latency on user experience is known as "client-side prediction" latency mitigation.

The term "latency" describes how long it takes for data to travel between a client and a server. Latency in networked applications can lead to lags in player actions or updates, which makes the user experience less fluid and responsive.

Code Example:

```
# Client-side prediction example
class Player:
    def __init__(self):
        self.x, self.y = 0, 0
```

```python
        self.velocity_x, self.velocity_y = 0, 0

    def update_position(self, time_delta):
        # Update position based on velocity and time delta
        self.x += self.velocity_x * time_delta
        self.y += self.velocity_y * time_delta

# Game loop on the client side
current_time = get_current_time()
previous_time = current_time

while True:
    # Calculate time delta
    current_time = get_current_time()
    time_delta = current_time - previous_time
    previous_time = current_time

    # Update player position using client-side prediction
    player.update_position(time_delta)

    # Render the game
    render_game()
```

Synchronizing Game State Between Clients and Server:

Making sure that every client connected to the server has current, consistent information about the game world and its entities is part of synchronizing game state between clients and the server.

In multiplayer games, keeping the game state synchronized is essential to giving each player an even and consistent gameplay experience. It entails monitoring several game elements, including player positions, object placement, score, and other pertinent information.

Code Example:

```python
# State synchronization example
class MultiplayerServer:
    def __init__(self):
        self.game_state = {
            'players': {},
            # Add other game state information
        }

    def synchronize_state(self, client_socket):
        try:
            # Send the current game state to the client
            state_message = json.dumps(self.game_state)
            client_socket.send(state_message.encode('utf-8'))
        except Exception as e:
            print(f"Error synchronizing state: {e}")

# On the client side
class MultiplayerClient:
    def synchronize_state(self):
        try:
            # Receive and update the game state from the server
            data = self.client_socket.recv(1024)
            state_message = data.decode('utf-8')
            game_state = json.loads(state_message)

            # Update local game state
            self.update_local_state(game_state)
        except Exception as e:
            print(f"Error synchronizing state: {e}")
```

Implementing Anti-Cheating Measures:

Integrating security methods and procedures into a software program or game to stop or identify player cheating is known as "implementing anti-cheating measures."

Unauthorized and unfair methods that provide players with an unfair edge or obstruct the intended gameplay experience are referred to as cheating. It can involve actions like hacking, taking advantage of security holes, utilizing third-party software or cheats, or altering game data.

Code Example:

```python
# Anti-cheating example
class MultiplayerServer:
    def validate_movement(self, player_id, new_position):
        # Check if the movement is valid based on game rules
        # Add additional checks as needed

        # Update the player's position if the movement is valid
        self.game_state['players'][player_id]['position'] =
        new_position

# On the client side
class MultiplayerClient:
    def send_movement(self, new_position):
        try:
# Send the proposed movement to the server for
validation
movement_message = {'action': 'move', 'new_position':
new_position}
self.client_socket.send(json.dumps(movement_message).encode('utf-8'))
        except Exception as e:
            print(f"Error sending movement: {e}")
```

It is important to give careful thought to problems like cheating prevention, state synchronization, and latency while addressing challenges in online gaming. The given code snippets show how to apply anti-cheating mechanisms, synchronize game state between clients and servers, and reduce latency through client-side prediction. These tips will help you make your Python multiplayer games more engaging and entertaining as you develop them.

Game Design Principles

Understanding Key Game Design Concepts

For games to be immersive and interesting for players, effective game design is essential. We'll explore important game design ideas in this chapter and offer examples of Python code to show how they're put into practice.

Player Input and Controls:

In game creation, player input and controls are crucial elements that define how users engage with the game. They let users explore, engage with, and take control of different parts of the virtual environment. This covers actions like attacking, using objects, or interacting with them, as well as controls for mobility like sprinting, jumping, or walking.

Code Example:

```python
# Player input example using Pygame
import pygame

# Initialize Pygame
pygame.init()

# Set up the game window
window_size = (800, 600)
```

```python
screen = pygame.display.set_mode(window_size)
pygame.display.set_caption("Player Input Example")

# Game loop
running = True
while running:
    for event in pygame.event.get():
        if event.type == pygame.QUIT:
            running = False
        elif event.type == pygame.KEYDOWN:
            if event.key == pygame.K_LEFT:
                # Handle left arrow key press
                print("Left arrow key pressed")
            elif event.key == pygame.K_RIGHT:
                # Handle right arrow key press
                print("Right arrow key pressed")

    # Update game state and render

    pygame.display.flip()

# Quit Pygame
pygame.quit()
```

Game Physics and Simulations:

The essential elements of game creation that provide virtual worlds realism and interactivity are game physics and simulations. To produce realistic movement, collisions, and interactions inside the gaming environment, they simulate physical laws and behaviors.

To compute and simulate the motion, forces, and interactions of objects in the game environment, game physics engines are utilized. To guarantee that items behave properly, these engines take into account variables like gravity, friction, velocity, acceleration, and collision detection. This improves the immersion and gameplay experience by enabling realistic movement of people, objects, and scenery.

Code Example:

```python
# Simple physics simulation example
class Particle:
    def __init__(self, x, y, mass):
        self.x = x
        self.y = y
        self.mass = mass
        self.velocity_x = 0
        self.velocity_y = 0

    def apply_force(self, force_x, force_y):
        # Calculate acceleration based on Newton's second law (F
        = ma)
        acceleration_x = force_x / self.mass
        acceleration_y = force_y / self.mass

        # Update velocity based on acceleration
        self.velocity_x += acceleration_x
        self.velocity_y += acceleration_y

        # Update position based on velocity
        self.x += self.velocity_x
        self.y += self.velocity_y

# Example usage
particle = Particle(0, 0, 1)
particle.apply_force(2, 0.5)
```

Game Graphics and Rendering:

Game graphics and rendering, which deal with producing and showcasing re
alistic and aesthetically pleasing images in a game, are essential components
of game development.

The visual components of a game, such as the characters, objects, environments, textures, and special effects, are referred to as game graphics. A variety
of methods, including 3D modeling, texturing, shading, and animation, are

used to create these visuals. Making visually appealing and engaging game environments that enthrall players is the aim.

Code Example:

```python
# Simple graphics rendering using Pygame
import pygame

# Initialize Pygame
pygame.init()

# Set up the game window
window_size = (800, 600)
screen = pygame.display.set_mode(window_size)
pygame.display.set_caption("Graphics Rendering Example")

# Game loop
running = True
while running:
    for event in pygame.event.get():
        if event.type == pygame.QUIT:
            running = False

    # Clear the screen
    screen.fill((255, 255, 255))

    # Draw shapes, sprites, and images

    # Update game state and render

    pygame.display.flip()

# Quit Pygame
pygame.quit()
```

Game Audio and Sound Effects:

The term "game audio" describes how sound is used in video games, such as sound effects, background music, and ambient noises. It enhances the game world's depth, ambiance, and feelings, giving gamers a more engaging experience.

Certain audio cues known as "sound effects" are used to enhance certain in-game interactions, events, or actions. These can include sounds from footsteps, weapons, explosions, the environment, and a variety of other audio components that improve the game's realism and informational value.

Code Example:

```python
# Simple audio playback using Pygame
import pygame

# Initialize Pygame
pygame.init()

# Set up the game window (not required for audio playback)
window_size = (800, 600)
screen = pygame.display.set_mode(window_size)

# Load a sound file
sound = pygame.mixer.Sound("example_sound.wav")

# Play the sound
sound.play()

# Wait for the sound to finish playing
pygame.time.wait(int(sound.get_length() * 1000))

# Quit Pygame
pygame.quit()
```

User Interface (UI) and Menus:

The menus, buttons, icons, HUD (Heads-Up Display), and other on-screen components are all included in the user interface, which is the collection of visual elements and controls that players use to interact with the game. By acting as a link between the player and the game, it gives them access to data, settings, and features.

Code Example:

```python
# Simple UI using Pygame
import pygame

# Initialize Pygame
pygame.init()

# Set up the game window
window_size = (800, 600)
screen = pygame.display.set_mode(window_size)
pygame.display.set_caption("UI Example")

# Create a button class
class Button:
    def __init__(self, x, y, width, height, text):
        self.rect = pygame.Rect(x, y, width, height)
        self.text = text

    def draw(self, surface):
        pygame.draw.rect(surface, (255, 0, 0), self.rect)
        font = pygame.font.Font(None, 36)
        text = font.render(self.text, True, (255, 255, 255))
        surface.blit(text, (self.rect.centerx - text.get_width()
        // 2, self.rect.centery - text.get_height() // 2))

# Create a button instance
play_button = Button(300, 200, 200, 50, "Play")

# Game loop
running = True
while running:
    for event in pygame.event.get():
        if event.type == pygame.QUIT:
            running = False
        elif event.type == pygame.MOUSEBUTTONDOWN:
```

```python
            if event.button == 1:  # Left mouse button
                if play_button.rect.collidepoint(event.pos):
                    # Handle play button click
                    print("Play button clicked")

        # Clear the screen
        screen.fill((255, 255, 255))

        # Draw UI elements
        play_button.draw(screen)

        # Update game state and render

        pygame.display.flip()

# Quit Pygame
pygame.quit()
```

Comprehending these fundamental principles of game design is important for crafting captivating and delightful Python games. The code snippets that are supplied provide useful illustrations to assist you in incorporating these ideas into your projects and improving the overall gaming experience for your gamers.

Applying Principles for Engaging Gameplay

Any good game must have gameplay that is compelling. This section will cover the ideas and methods for utilizing Python to make engaging and immersive gaming experiences. These principles are put into practice in the accompanying code samples.

Player Feedback and Responsiveness:

The data and hints that players receive in response to their activities and interactions in the game are referred to as player feedback. This can be in the form of auditory feedback like music or sound effects, visual feedback like animations or effects, and haptic feedback like vibration or controller rumble. Feedback encourages participation, offers direction, and aids in players' understanding of the effects of their actions.

Conversely, responsiveness describes how fast and precisely a game reacts to inputs from the player. A game that is responsive guarantees that player actions are recorded and carried out promptly, resulting in a fluid and easy-to-play gameplay experience. To make sure that players feel in control and fully involved in the game, it entails eliminating input lag, maximizing performance, and keeping a high frame rate.

Code Example:

```python
# Player feedback example using Pygame
import pygame

# Initialize Pygame
pygame.init()

# Set up the game window
window_size = (800, 600)
screen = pygame.display.set_mode(window_size)
pygame.display.set_caption("Player Feedback Example")

# Load an image for feedback
feedback_image = pygame.image.load("feedback.png")

# Game loop
running = True
while running:
    for event in pygame.event.get():
        if event.type == pygame.QUIT:
            running = False

    # Clear the screen
    screen.fill((255, 255, 255))
```

```
    # Draw game elements

    # Provide visual feedback
    screen.blit(feedback_image, (300, 200))

    # Update game state and render

    pygame.display.flip()

  # Quit Pygame
  pygame.quit()
```

Balancing and Pacing:

In order to provide fair and entertaining gameplay, balancing refers to the process of modifying different parts of the game, such as character abilities, weaponry, difficulty levels, and resource distribution. It entails adjusting the game's mechanisms to provide a sense of difficulty and advancement while averting overly simple or complex circumstances. For players of various skill levels to have a fulfilling and interesting experience, balancing is essential.

Contrarily, pacing describes the cadence and flow of the game. To keep players interested and avoid boredom, player interactions such as fight encounters, puzzles, and story moments are all controlled in terms of pace and intensity. By alternating between tense, exciting, and relaxing periods, pacing contributes to the creation of a dynamic and captivating experience.

Code Example:

```
  # Game balancing and pacing example
  class Enemy:
      def __init__(self, health, damage):
          self.health = health
          self.damage = damage
```

```python
# Balancing adjustments
enemy_easy = Enemy(50, 10)
enemy_medium = Enemy(75, 15)
enemy_hard = Enemy(100, 20)

# Pacing adjustments
def increase_difficulty(level):
    # Increase enemy health and damage based on the game level
    return Enemy(level * 25, level * 5)

# Example usage
current_game_level = 1
current_enemy = increase_difficulty(current_game_level)
```

Reward Systems and Achievements:

Reward systems are in-game mechanics that give players material or immaterial prizes for accomplishing particular missions or reaching predetermined objectives. These incentives may take the form of in-game cash, gear, boosts, access to unlocked content, or even just a feeling of accomplishment. Reward programs are made to inspire players, promote participation, and improve the entire gaming experience.

Conversely, achievements are certain objectives or benchmarks that players can work toward while playing a game. They could include finishing story objectives, hitting particular scores or levels, finding hidden secrets, or becoming an expert at a particular gameplay mechanic. Rewards for achievements can include in-game accolades, trophies, badges, or other items. They provide gamers a feeling of difficulty, advancement, and success.

Code Example:

```python
# Reward system and achievements example
class Player:
```

```python
    def __init__(self):
        self.score = 0
        self.level = 1

    def earn_points(self, points):
        # Increase player score based on points earned
        self.score += points

        # Check for level up
        if self.score >= self.level * 100:
            self.level_up()

    def level_up(self):
        # Increase player level and provide a reward
        self.level += 1
        print(f"Level up! You are now at level {self.level}")

 # Example usage
 player = Player()
 player.earn_points(50)
```

Dynamic and Evolving Gameplay:

The term "dynamic gameplay" describes responsive and flexible gaming systems and features that let the user choose and act in a way that creates a variety of experiences and outcomes. It entails building a dynamic, living game world that responds to choices made by the player, giving them a sense of agency and influence. Players are kept interested in dynamic gaming because it provides diversity, surprise, and chances for experimentation and discovery.

On the other hand, evolving gameplay entails making gradual modifications and updates to the game. This can involve adding new features, material, challenges, or even changing the story or gameplay mechanics of the game. Gamers are encouraged to keep playing and investigating the game long after it has been released since the gameplay is constantly evolving, keeping the experience engaging and new.

Code Example:

```python
# Dynamic and evolving gameplay example using Pygame
import pygame

# Initialize Pygame
pygame.init()

# Set up the game window
window_size = (800, 600)
screen = pygame.display.set_mode(window_size)
pygame.display.set_caption("Dynamic Gameplay Example")

# Game variables
player_speed = 5
enemy_speed = 3
player_x, player_y = 400, 300

# Game loop
running = True
while running:
    for event in pygame.event.get():
        if event.type == pygame.QUIT:
            running = False

    # Handle player input
    keys = pygame.key.get_pressed()
    if keys[pygame.K_LEFT]:
        player_x -= player_speed
    if keys[pygame.K_RIGHT]:
        player_x += player_speed
    if keys[pygame.K_UP]:
        player_y -= player_speed
    if keys[pygame.K_DOWN]:
        player_y += player_speed

    # Update game state
    # Add dynamic elements and events

    # Clear the screen
```

```python
    screen.fill((255, 255, 255))

    # Draw game elements
    pygame.draw.rect(screen, (0, 0, 255), (player_x, player_y,
    50, 50))

    # Update game state and render

    pygame.display.flip()

# Quit Pygame
pygame.quit()
```

Narrative and Storytelling:

The term "narrative" describes the game's main plot, which includes the characters, location, and events. It gives the player's journey a structure and acts as the inspiration for their decisions and actions in the game. A compelling story draws players in, stirs up feelings, and gives the gameplay experience more nuance and significance.

The strategies and procedures utilized to present the story to the players are all included in storytelling. This can involve conversations, cutscenes, in-game activities, narratives from the environment, and more. Good narrative strategies improve player engagement, assist immerse players in the game world, and provide memorable experiences.

Code Example:

```python
# Narrative and storytelling example
class DialogueSystem:
    def __init__(self):
        self.dialogue_tree = {
            'start': "Welcome to the game! What is your name?",
            'name_question': "Nice to meet you, {name}! Ready for
```

```python
        an adventure?"
    }

def start_dialogue(self):
    current_node = 'start'
    print(self.dialogue_tree[current_node])

    # Simulate player input
    player_name = input("Enter your name: ")
    self.dialogue_tree['name_question'] = f"Nice to meet you,
    {player_name}! Ready for an adventure?"

    current_node = 'name_question'
    print(self.dialogue_tree[current_node])

# Example usage
dialogue_system = DialogueSystem()
dialogue_system.start_dialogue()
```

You may increase player engagement and satisfaction in your Python games by implementing these ideas and tactics. These code snippets show you how to add reward systems, dynamic gameplay, player feedback, pace and balance your game, and combine storylines for a more engaging player experience.

Balancing and Refining Game Elements

A well-rounded and pleasurable gaming experience requires careful consideration and adjustment of game aspects. This section looks at methods and sample Python code to help you achieve balance and improve your game in a number of areas.

Balancing Enemy Attributes:

In order to provide fair and difficult gameplay, it's important to balance enemy attributes, which entails changing the traits and skills of foes.

The term "enemy attributes" describes a variety of characteristics that opponents in a game may have, including defense, speed, damage output, health, and special abilities. It's crucial to strike a balance between these characteristics to give gamers a fair and interesting fighting experience. It entails adjusting enemy stats to give a suitable degree of difficulty, making sure that opponents are neither too simple nor too tough to overcome.

Code Example:

```python
# Balancing enemy attributes example
class Enemy:
    def __init__(self, health, damage):
        self.health = health
        self.damage = damage

# Initial enemy attributes
basic_enemy = Enemy(50, 10)
strong_enemy = Enemy(100, 20)

# Adjusting attributes for balance
basic_enemy.health = 60
strong_enemy.damage = 25
```

Fine-Tuning Player Abilities:

In game development, player ability tuning is a painstaking process that goes into creating a fair and interesting gaming environment. Game developers concentrate on fine-tuning the player skills' efficacy, range, and constraints to make sure they mesh well with the overall game design. Iterative testing, feedback analysis, and data-driven modifications are employed to attain the best possible player empowerment while maintaining the integrity of the game. Cooldown times, resource prices, and skill advancement are examples of fine-tuning that work together to give players a sense of mastery without making an ability feel too strong or too meek. Finding the ideal mix between providing players with a fair and fun challenge and promoting strategic thinking and good execution makes for dynamic and exciting gameplay.

Code Example:

```python
# Fine-tuning player abilities example
class Player:
    def __init__(self):
        self.health = 100
        self.attack_power = 15
        self.defense = 10

# Initial player abilities
player = Player()

# Fine-tuning for better balance
player.health = 120
player.attack_power = 18
player.defense = 12
```

Optimizing Resource Management:

A crucial component of game development is resource optimization, which entails effectively allocating and employing in-game resources.

The planned distribution and use of resources, such as money, objects, energy, or time, in a game is known as resource management. To advance in the game, players must carefully consider the acquisition, use, and replenishment of resources. Player agency, challenge, and gaming depth are all improved by efficient resource management.

Code Example:

```python
# Optimizing resource management example
class Player:
    def __init__(self):
        self.health = 100
        self.mana = 50
        self.stamina = 80
```

```python
    def use_ability(self, ability_cost):
        # Check if there's enough resource to use the ability
        if self.mana >= ability_cost:
            # Use the ability and consume the resource
            self.mana -= ability_cost
            print("Ability used successfully!")
        else:
            print("Not enough mana to use the ability.")

# Example usage
player = Player()
player.use_ability(30)  # Attempt to use an ability costing 30
mana
```

Adjusting Game Difficulty:

The degree of struggle and expertise needed to advance and succeed in a game is referred to as game difficulty. It's critical to balance game difficulty so that players of all skill levels may interact with the game and enjoy themselves. It entails modifying the power of the adversaries, the difficulty of the puzzles, the time constraints, the availability of resources, and the general gameplay mechanics.

Code Example:

```python
# Adjusting game difficulty example
class Enemy:
    def __init__(self, health, damage):
        self.health = health
        self.damage = damage

# Function to adjust enemy difficulty based on game level
def adjust_difficulty(enemy, game_level):
    enemy.health += game_level * 10
    enemy.damage += game_level * 5
```

```python
# Example usage
basic_enemy = Enemy(50, 10)
adjust_difficulty(basic_enemy, 3)  # Increase difficulty for game
level 3
```

Refining Animation Speed:

A crucial part of game development is refining animation speed, which entails timing and pacing animations to create a fluid and well-polished gameplay experience.

The pace at which objects, characters, or other visual components move and change during gameplay is referred to as animation speed. Developers may make sure that movements and transitions are responsive, aesthetically pleasing, and seem natural by fine-tuning animation speed.

Code Example:

```python
# Refining animation speed example using Pygame
import pygame

# Initialize Pygame
pygame.init()

# Set up the game window
window_size = (800, 600)
screen = pygame.display.set_mode(window_size)
pygame.display.set_caption("Animation Speed Example")

# Load an image for animation
character_image = pygame.image.load("character.png")

# Animation variables
animation_speed = 5
```

```python
character_x = 0

# Game loop
running = True
while running:
    for event in pygame.event.get():
        if event.type == pygame.QUIT:
            running = False

    # Update game state
    character_x += animation_speed

    # Clear the screen
    screen.fill((255, 255, 255))

    # Draw game elements with refined animation speed
    screen.blit(character_image, (character_x, 300))

    # Update and render

    pygame.display.flip()

# Quit Pygame
pygame.quit()
```

Iteration and testing are necessary to balance and improve game aspects. These examples show how to modify player and enemy attributes, manage resources more efficiently, modify difficulty settings, and improve animation speed. Making constant improvements to these components will help ensure that the gameplay in your Python games is balanced and fun.

Building a Complete Game Project

Integrating Various Concepts Learned

Let's create a thorough example that incorporates user input, game physics, graphics rendering, music, a user interface, and multiplayer functionality using Python and Pygame. This will incorporate every concept covered in this book. This example will show how these concepts combine to create an engaging and exciting game.

Complete Game Integration:

"Complete game integration," as used in the context of game creation, is the meticulous process of combining different elements—such as sounds, graphics, mechanics, and user interfaces—smoothly together to produce a seamless and captivating gaming environment. Making sure that every component functions as a whole is the aim of game development in order to provide a polished and coherent end product.

This means incorporating state-of-the-art technologies like as dynamic AI behaviors, responsive input systems, and multiplayer capability. Throughout the development process, a great deal of testing, optimization, and fine-tuning is done to address any possible issues and enhance the gameplay overall. The success of full game integration is determined by the ability to provide a seamless, enjoyable, and fully realized gaming experience that aligns with the developer's vision and captivates gamers from start to finish.

```python
# Full game integration example using Pygame
import pygame
import random
import socket
import threading

# Initialize Pygame
pygame.init()

# Set up the game window
window_size = (800, 600)
screen = pygame.display.set_mode(window_size)
pygame.display.set_caption("Integrated Python Game")

# Load images and sounds
player_image = pygame.image.load("player.png")
enemy_image = pygame.image.load("enemy.png")
explosion_sound = pygame.mixer.Sound("explosion.wav")

# Player class with basic physics
class Player:
    def __init__(self, x, y):
        self.x = x
        self.y = y
        self.velocity_x = 0
        self.velocity_y = 0

    def update_position(self):
        self.x += self.velocity_x
        self.y += self.velocity_y

# Enemy class with basic AI
class Enemy:
    def __init__(self, x, y):
        self.x = x
        self.y = y
        self.velocity_x = random.uniform(-2, 2)
        self.velocity_y = random.uniform(-2, 2)
```

```python
    def update_position(self):
        self.x += self.velocity_x
        self.y += self.velocity_y


# Networking components for multiplayer
class MultiplayerServer:
    def __init__(self):
        self.server_socket = socket.socket(socket.AF_INET,
        socket.SOCK_STREAM)
        self.server_socket.bind(('0.0.0.0', 5555))
        self.server_socket.listen()

        self.clients = []

        print("Server listening for incoming connections...")

    def start(self):
        while True:
            client_socket, _ = self.server_socket.accept()
            self.clients.append(client_socket)

            # Handle the client in a separate thread
            client_handler =
            threading.Thread(target=self.handle_client,
            args=(client_socket,))
            client_handler.start()

    def handle_client(self, client_socket):
        while True:
            try:
                # Receive and broadcast data
                data = client_socket.recv(1024)
                if not data:
                    break

                # Broadcast the message to all clients
                for client in self.clients:
                    if client != client_socket:
                        client.send(data)
```

```python
        except Exception as e:
            print(f"Error handling client: {e}")
            break

# Create player and enemy instances
player = Player(400, 500)
enemies = [Enemy(random.randint(50, 750), random.randint(50,
200)) for _ in range(5)]

# Initialize networking for multiplayer
server = MultiplayerServer()
network_thread = threading.Thread(target=server.start)
network_thread.start()

# Game loop
running = True
while running:
    for event in pygame.event.get():
        if event.type == pygame.QUIT:
            running = False

    # Handle player input
    keys = pygame.key.get_pressed()
    if keys[pygame.K_LEFT]:
        player.velocity_x = -3
    elif keys[pygame.K_RIGHT]:
        player.velocity_x = 3
    else:
        player.velocity_x = 0

    # Update game state
    player.update_position()
    for enemy in enemies:
        enemy.update_position()

    # Check for collisions
    for enemy in enemies:
        if pygame.Rect(player.x, player.y, 50,
        50).colliderect(pygame.Rect(enemy.x, enemy.y, 50, 50)):
            explosion_sound.play()
```

```python
    # Clear the screen
    screen.fill((255, 255, 255))

    # Draw game elements
    screen.blit(player_image, (player.x, player.y))
    for enemy in enemies:
        screen.blit(enemy_image, (enemy.x, enemy.y))

    # Update and render

    pygame.display.flip()

# Quit Pygame
pygame.quit()
```

This example integrates key concepts learned throughout the book, including player input, game physics, graphics rendering, audio, UI, and multiplayer functionality. The result is a comprehensive Python game that showcases the synergy of these concepts to create an engaging and dynamic gaming experience.

Developing a Polished and Complete Game

A polished and comprehensive game must improve and refine a number of elements, such as the user interface, gaming mechanics, audio, graphics, and overall user experience. This section offers guidance on utilizing Python and Pygame to produce a polished end product, along with code samples to highlight important ideas.

Enhanced Graphics with Sprites:

In game creation, sprites are used to improve graphics by using 2D bitmap images to improve visual quality and attractiveness. To save RAM and improve rendering speed, developers use sprite sheets and atlases to effectively manage several images in a single file.

Sprites are used to create dynamic character movements, fluid animations, and a variety of visual effects by altering their frames or attributes over time. This method is very common in 2D games since it makes it possible to create environments that are both visually appealing and detailed, all while utilizing resources in an effective manner. The incorporation of sprites improves the overall quality of the graphics, making the game more visually captivating and immersive.

```python
# Enhanced graphics example using Pygame sprites
import pygame

# Initialize Pygame
pygame.init()

# Set up the game window
window_size = (800, 600)
screen = pygame.display.set_mode(window_size)
pygame.display.set_caption("Polished Game Graphics")

# Create a sprite class
class Player(pygame.sprite.Sprite):
    def __init__(self):
        super().__init__()
        self.image = pygame.image.load("player_sprite.png")
        self.rect = self.image.get_rect()
        self.rect.center = (window_size[0] // 2, window_size[1]
        // 2)

# Create sprite groups
all_sprites = pygame.sprite.Group()
player_sprite = Player()
all_sprites.add(player_sprite)

# Game loop
running = True
while running:
    for event in pygame.event.get():
        if event.type == pygame.QUIT:
```

```
        running = False

    # Update game state

    # Clear the screen
    screen.fill((255, 255, 255))

    # Draw sprites
    all_sprites.draw(screen)

    # Update and render

    pygame.display.flip()

# Quit Pygame
pygame.quit()
```

Immersive Audio Experience:

It takes careful work to integrate dynamic audio technologies, spatial audio, and excellent sound design to provide an immersive audio experience in a game. To improve the mood and narrative of the game, developers use a blend of music, interactive sound effects, and ambient noises. By adding a sense of depth and directionality, spatial audio techniques like 3D sound positioning enhance the player's experience of the virtual world.

In response to in-game events, dynamic audio systems make sure that soundscapes change organically in response to player choices and the story as it progresses. In addition to enhancing the visual components, a well-executed immersive audio experience is essential to generating an engaging and emotionally impactful gaming environment.

```
# Immersive audio experience using Pygame
import pygame

# Initialize Pygame
```

```python
pygame.init()

# Set up the game window
window_size = (800, 600)
screen = pygame.display.set_mode(window_size)
pygame.display.set_caption("Immersive Audio Experience")

# Load background music
pygame.mixer.music.load("background_music.mp3")
pygame.mixer.music.play(-1)  # Loop the music

# Load sound effects
explosion_sound = pygame.mixer.Sound("explosion.wav")

# Game loop
running = True
while running:
    for event in pygame.event.get():
        if event.type == pygame.QUIT:
            running = False

        # Trigger sound effect on key press
        if event.type == pygame.KEYDOWN and event.key ==
        pygame.K_SPACE:
            explosion_sound.play()

    # Update game state

    # Clear the screen
    screen.fill((255, 255, 255))

    # Update and render

    pygame.display.flip()

# Quit Pygame
pygame.quit()
```

Polished User Interface with Pygame GUI:

```python
# Polished user interface using Pygame GUI
import pygame
from pygame_gui import UIManager, elements

# Initialize Pygame
pygame.init()

# Set up the game window
window_size = (800, 600)
screen = pygame.display.set_mode(window_size)
pygame.display.set_caption("Polished User Interface")

# Create a UI manager
ui_manager = UIManager(window_size)

# Create a button
button = elements.UIButton(relative_rect=pygame.Rect((350, 275),
(100, 50)),
                                text='Click Me!',
                                manager=ui_manager)

# Game loop
running = True
while running:
    for event in pygame.event.get():
        if event.type == pygame.QUIT:
            running = False

        # Process UI events
        if event.type == pygame.USEREVENT:
            if event.user_type == pygame_gui.UI_BUTTON_PRESSED:
                if event.ui_element == button:
                    print('Button Clicked!')

        ui_manager.process_events(event)

    # Update game state

    # Clear the screen
    screen.fill((255, 255, 255))
```

```python
    # Draw UI elements
    ui_manager.draw_ui(screen)

    # Update and render

    pygame.display.flip()

# Quit Pygame
pygame.quit()
```

Refined Gameplay Mechanics:

The goal of fine-tuning gameplay mechanics in game development is to maximize the essential interactive components of a game through painstaking, iterative process. To produce a harmonic and captivating experience, developers concentrate on optimizing user controls, balancing character powers, and tweaking game regulations. Playtesting, feedback analysis, and data-driven modifications are all part of this process to make sure the mechanics meet the desired design objectives.

Achieving a delicate balance that offers challenge, rewards talent, and upholds justice is crucial when refining gameplay mechanics, which span from level designs and combat systems to economies and progression structures. The capacity of well-developed gameplay mechanisms to provide a fulfilling, engaging, and joyful experience that enthralls players and keeps them invested in the gaming journey is what makes them successful.

```python
# Refined gameplay mechanics example using Pygame
import pygame

# Initialize Pygame
pygame.init()
```

```python
# Set up the game window
window_size = (800, 600)
screen = pygame.display.set_mode(window_size)
pygame.display.set_caption("Refined Gameplay Mechanics")

# Create a player class with advanced mechanics
class Player(pygame.sprite.Sprite):
    def __init__(self):
        super().__init__()
        self.image = pygame.image.load("player_sprite.png")
        self.rect = self.image.get_rect()
        self.rect.center = (window_size[0] // 2, window_size[1]
        // 2)
        self.speed = 5

    def update(self):
        keys = pygame.key.get_pressed()
        if keys[pygame.K_LEFT]:
            self.rect.x -= self.speed
        if keys[pygame.K_RIGHT]:
            self.rect.x += self.speed
        if keys[pygame.K_UP]:
            self.rect.y -= self.speed
        if keys[pygame.K_DOWN]:
            self.rect.y += self.speed

# Create sprite groups
all_sprites = pygame.sprite.Group()
player_sprite = Player()
all_sprites.add(player_sprite)

# Game loop
running = True
while running:
    for event in pygame.event.get():
        if event.type == pygame.QUIT:
            running = False

    # Update game state
    all_sprites.update()
```

```python
    # Clear the screen
    screen.fill((255, 255, 255))

    # Draw sprites
    all_sprites.draw(screen)

    # Update and render

    pygame.display.flip()

  # Quit Pygame
  pygame.quit()
```

It takes careful consideration of the user interface, gaming mechanics, audio, graphics, and other details to create a polished and comprehensive game. These code samples show off how to employ sprites to improve graphics, produce a rich audio experience, craft a well-designed user interface, and improve gameplay dynamics. Putting these components together will result in a finished work that is compelling and well-written.

The Art of Game Finishing Touches

A polished and comprehensive game requires final touches that improve the user experience as a whole. This section examines the essential components of game production that go into creating a polished and captivating end result. The accompanying code snippets demonstrate how to use Pygame and Python to implement these last touches.

Dynamic Lighting Effects:

Implementing dynamic lighting effects can add depth and realism to your game. This example showcases dynamic lighting around a player-controlled character.

```python
import pygame
import random

# Initialize Pygame
pygame.init()

# Set up the game window
window_size = (800, 600)
screen = pygame.display.set_mode(window_size)
pygame.display.set_caption("Dynamic Lighting Effects")

# Create a player class
class Player(pygame.sprite.Sprite):
    def __init__(self, x, y):
        super().__init__()
        self.image = pygame.Surface((50, 50))
        self.image.fill((255, 255, 255))
        self.rect = self.image.get_rect()
        self.rect.center = (x, y)

# Create a sprite group for the player
all_sprites = pygame.sprite.Group()
player = Player(window_size[0] // 2, window_size[1] // 2)
all_sprites.add(player)

# Game loop
running = True
while running:
    for event in pygame.event.get():
        if event.type == pygame.QUIT:
            running = False

    # Clear the screen
    screen.fill((0, 0, 0))

    # Draw dynamic lighting effect
    pygame.draw.circle(screen, (255, 255, 255),
    player.rect.center, 100, 10)

    # Draw player
```

```
    all_sprites.draw(screen)

    # Update and render
    pygame.display.flip()

# Quit Pygame
pygame.quit()
```

Smooth Transitions and Animations:

Smooth transitions and animations enhance the overall fluidity of your game. This example demonstrates smooth movement transitions for a player-controlled character.

```
import pygame

# Initialize Pygame
pygame.init()

# Set up the game window
window_size = (800, 600)
screen = pygame.display.set_mode(window_size)
pygame.display.set_caption("Smooth Transitions and Animations")

# Create a player class with smooth movement
class Player(pygame.sprite.Sprite):
    def __init__(self):
        super().__init__()
        self.image = pygame.Surface((50, 50))
        self.image.fill((255, 0, 0))
        self.rect = self.image.get_rect()
        self.rect.center = (window_size[0] // 2, window_size[1]
        // 2)
        self.target_x = window_size[0] // 2
        self.target_y = window_size[1] // 2

    def update(self):
        # Smoothly move towards the target position
```

```python
        speed = 3
        self.rect.x += (self.target_x - self.rect.x) / speed
        self.rect.y += (self.target_y - self.rect.y) / speed

# Create a sprite group for the player
all_sprites = pygame.sprite.Group()
player = Player()
all_sprites.add(player)

# Game loop
running = True
while running:
    for event in pygame.event.get():
        if event.type == pygame.QUIT:
            running = False

        # Set a new target position on mouse click
        if event.type == pygame.MOUSEBUTTONDOWN:
            player.target_x, player.target_y = 
            pygame.mouse.get_pos()

    # Clear the screen
    screen.fill((255, 255, 255))

    # Draw player
    all_sprites.draw(screen)

    # Update and render
    all_sprites.update()
    pygame.display.flip()

# Quit Pygame
pygame.quit()
```

Particle Effects for Visual Appeal:

Particle effects can add excitement and visual appeal to your game. This example demonstrates a simple particle system for explosions.

```python
import pygame
import random

# Initialize Pygame
pygame.init()

# Set up the game window
window_size = (800, 600)
screen = pygame.display.set_mode(window_size)
pygame.display.set_caption("Particle Effects for Visual Appeal")

# Create a particle class for visual effects
class Particle(pygame.sprite.Sprite):
    def __init__(self, x, y):
        super().__init__()
        self.image = pygame.Surface((5, 5))
        self.image.fill((random.randint(0, 255),
        random.randint(0, 255), random.randint(0, 255)))
        self.rect = self.image.get_rect()
        self.rect.center = (x, y)
        self.velocity_x = random.uniform(-2, 2)
        self.velocity_y = random.uniform(-2, 2)
        self.lifetime = 100

    def update(self):
        self.rect.x += self.velocity_x
        self.rect.y += self.velocity_y
        self.lifetime -= 1
        if self.lifetime <= 0:
            self.kill()

# Create a sprite group for particles
particles = pygame.sprite.Group()

# Game loop
running = True
while running:
    for event in pygame.event.get():
        if event.type == pygame.QUIT:
            running = False
```

```python
    # Spawn particles on mouse click
    mouse_x, mouse_y = pygame.mouse.get_pos()
    if pygame.mouse.get_pressed()[0]:
        for _ in range(5):
            particle = Particle(mouse_x, mouse_y)
            particles.add(particle)

    # Clear the screen
    screen.fill((255, 255, 255))

    # Draw particles
    particles.draw(screen)

    # Update particle positions
    particles.update()

    # Update and render
    pygame.display.flip()

# Quit Pygame
pygame.quit()
```

User-Friendly Menus and Feedback:

Creating user-friendly menus and providing clear feedback enhances the overall user experience. This example demonstrates the implementation of a simple start menu using Pygame GUI.

```python
import pygame
from pygame_gui import UIManager, elements

# Initialize Pygame
pygame.init()

# Set up the game window
window_size = (800, 600)
screen = pygame.display.set_mode(window_size)
```

```python
pygame.display.set_caption("User-Friendly Menus and Feedback")

# Create a UI manager
ui_manager = UIManager(window_size)

# Create UI elements for menus
start_button = elements.UIButton(relative_rect=pygame.Rect((350,
275), (100, 50)),
                                 text='Start',
                                 manager=ui_manager)

quit_button = elements.UIButton(relative_rect=pygame.Rect((350,
350), (100, 50)),
                                 text='Quit',
                                 manager=ui_manager)

# Game loop
running = True
while running:
    for event in pygame.event.get():
        if event.type == pygame.QUIT:
            running = False

        # Process UI events
        if event.type == pygame.USEREVENT:
            if event.user_type == pygame_gui.UI_BUTTON_PRESSED:
                if event.ui_element == start_button:
                    print('Game Started!')
                elif event.ui_element == quit_button:
                    running = False

        ui_manager.process_events(event)

    # Clear the screen
    screen.fill((255, 255, 255))

    # Draw UI elements
    ui_manager.draw_ui(screen)

    # Update and render
```

```
    pygame.display.flip()

# Quit Pygame
pygame.quit()
```

These code samples demonstrate how important final touches are implemented in games; they include particle effects, user-friendly menus, smooth transitions and animations, and dynamic lighting effects. You may make your game more polished and comprehensive by using these components, giving gamers an engaging and entertaining gaming experience.

A Sample Game

Galactic Defender: A Space Shooter Game

Game Concept:

Galactic Defender is a 2D space shooter where the player takes control of a spacecraft tasked with defending the galaxy against waves of alien invaders. The game features dynamic gameplay, smooth controls, and incorporates elements such as dynamic lighting, smooth animations, particle effects, and user-friendly menus.

Below is the python code for the game:

```
import pygame
import random

# Initialize Pygame
pygame.init()

# Set up the game window
window_size = (800, 600)
screen = pygame.display.set_mode(window_size)
```

```python
pygame.display.set_caption("Galactic Defender")

# Define colors
WHITE = (255, 255, 255)
RED = (255, 0, 0)

# Create player class
class Player(pygame.sprite.Sprite):
    def __init__(self):
        super().__init__()
        self.image = pygame.Surface((50, 50))
        self.image.fill(WHITE)
        self.rect = self.image.get_rect()
        self.rect.center = (window_size[0] // 2, window_size[1] -
        50)

    def update(self):
        keys = pygame.key.get_pressed()
        if keys[pygame.K_LEFT] and self.rect.left > 0:
            self.rect.x -= 5
        if keys[pygame.K_RIGHT] and self.rect.right <
        window_size[0]:
            self.rect.x += 5

# Create enemy class
class Enemy(pygame.sprite.Sprite):
    def __init__(self):
        super().__init__()
        self.image = pygame.Surface((30, 30))
        self.image.fill(RED)
        self.rect = self.image.get_rect()
        self.rect.x = random.randrange(window_size[0] -
        self.rect.width)
        self.rect.y = random.randrange(-100, -40)
        self.speed_y = random.randrange(1, 5)

    def update(self):
        self.rect.y += self.speed_y
        if self.rect.top > window_size[1] + 10 or self.rect.right
        < 0 or self.rect.left > window_size[0]:
```

```python
        self.rect.x = random.randrange(window_size[0] -
            self.rect.width)
        self.rect.y = random.randrange(-100, -40)
        self.speed_y = random.randrange(1, 5)

# Create sprite groups
all_sprites = pygame.sprite.Group()
enemies = pygame.sprite.Group()
player = Player()
all_sprites.add(player)

# Game loop
running = True
clock = pygame.time.Clock()
spawn_counter = 0

while running:
    for event in pygame.event.get():
        if event.type == pygame.QUIT:
            running = False

    # Update
    all_sprites.update()

    # Check for collisions
    hits = pygame.sprite.spritecollide(player, enemies, False)
    if hits:
        running = False

    # Spawn enemies
    spawn_counter += 1
    if spawn_counter == 60:
        enemy = Enemy()
        all_sprites.add(enemy)
        enemies.add(enemy)
        spawn_counter = 0

    # Draw
    screen.fill((0, 0, 0))
    all_sprites.draw(screen)
```

```python
    # Refresh the screen
    pygame.display.flip()

    # Cap the frame rate
    clock.tick(60)

# Quit Pygame
pygame.quit()
```

The above code has the output shown below:

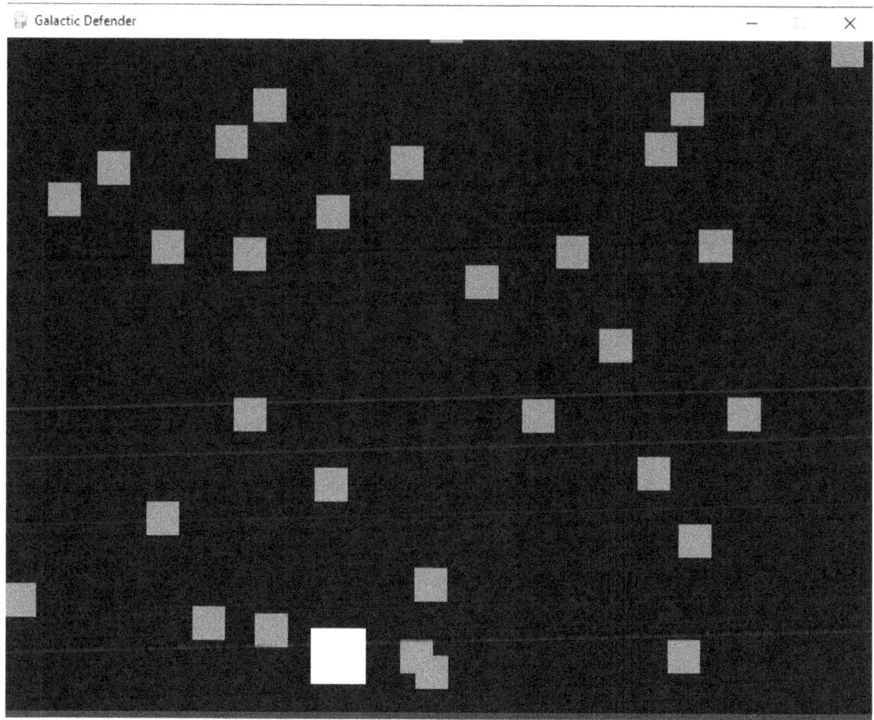

In this comprehensive journey through Python game programming, we've explored essential concepts and implemented key features to craft a captivating and polished python game. Hope the knowledge in this book was helpful to you.

****

Stay tuned for the second edition

****

About the Author

E. Jarrel is a college teacher who teaches computer programming courses. He has been writing programs since he was 15 years old. Jarrel currently focuses on writing software that addresses inefficiencies in education and brings the benefits of open source software to the field of education. In his spare time he enjoys climbing mountains and spending time with his family.

Also by Jarrel E.

C++ for Game Developers: Building Scalable and Robust Gaming Applications

Embark on a comprehensive journey through the intricacies of C++ for game development with this expertly crafted guide. Tailored for advanced programmers, this book serves as a definitive resource for building scalable and robust gaming applications.

From Zero to Java Hero: Master The Art of Java Programming

From Zero to Java Hero: Master the Art of Programming is a comprehensive guide designed to empower aspiring programmers with the knowledge and skills needed to excel in the world of Java development.

Python Mastery Unleashed: Advanced Programming Techniques

Python Mastery Unleashed: Advanced Programming Techniques is a comprehensive guide to mastering advanced programming techniques in Python. Designed for seasoned Python developers and aspiring programmers alike, this book offers a comprehensive understanding of the advanced programming techniques used by experienced Python developers to build complex systems and applications.

Python for Data Science: A Practical Approach to Machine Learning

Dive into the world of data science with Python for Data Science: A Practical Approach to Machine Learning. This comprehensive guide is meticulously crafted to provide you with the knowledge and skills necessary to excel in the ever-evolving field of data science.

www.ingramcontent.com/pod-product-compliance
Lightning Source LLC
Chambersburg PA
CBHW071419150726
48000CB00001B/402